CHANCTONBURY RING

The Story of a Sussex Landmark

Janet Pennington

Downland His...

*To my sister Pamela, and in memory
of my parents Eric and Hilda Holden*

Published by Downland History Publishing
5 Swallowmead, College Hill, Steyning, West Sussex BN44 3HE

Prepared for publication by Pomegranate Press
51 St Nicholas Lane, Lewes, Sussex www.pomegranate-press.co.uk

ISBN: 978 0 9555703 2 2

Front cover: 'Chenkbury [sic] Ring from the Downs near Steyning.' Sketched
1820, by W. H. Brooke (courtesy of Sussex Archaeological Society)

Title page: Chanctonbury Ring, South Downs, 1883, by A. Elliott (courtesy of
West Sussex County Council Library Service)

Back cover: Chanctonbury Ring across the River Adur, south-west of Henfield

British Library Cataloguing-in-Publication Data.
A catalogue record for this book is available from the British Library

CONTENTS

About the author

Janet Pennington, born in Sussex, is a regional historian with a PhD in early-modern inn and tavern history. Her MA dissertation was about the history of Wiston House and the life of Sir Thomas Sherley (*c.* 1542–1612), the owner and builder of the house tucked under the South Downs to the north-east of Chanctonbury Ring. In 1978 she joined the Wiston Estate Study Group, led by Roy Armstrong who founded the Weald & Downland Open Air Museum at Singleton; she was secretary of the Group for many years while they recorded the agricultural buildings and farmhouses on the estate. She is one of the five members of the 'Wiston History Girls' (listed in Acknowledgements). She is a member of the Wealden Buildings Study Group, who record and study vernacular architecture in south-east England, and is a member of council of the Sussex Record Society.

Janet was the archivist at Lancing College, an independent school in West Sussex, for eighteen years until she retired in 2004. She gives illustrated talks throughout Sussex, particularly on pubs (inns, taverns and alehouses), Wiston House and a variety of other subjects, such as the ritual protection of the home: a list is available on request which, of course, now includes a talk on the history of Chanctonbury Ring. With local historian Joyce Sleight she has spent over thirty years researching the history of Steyning, holding classes and leading walks around the historic streets of the medieval town. They have both published numerous articles. Janet taught local history and palaeography for the Centre of Continuing Education (now the Centre for Community Engagement) at the University of Sussex for twenty years. She lives in Steyning with her husband, and is always pleased to have enquiries from researchers by email: *jpsussex@hotmail.com*

Notes on transcription

In quoting from original sources, I have retained the spelling and capitalisation, but extended contemporary contractions. Dates are given in New Style, with the year regarded as beginning on 1 January.

Illustrations and Credits

Abbreviations
SAC – *Sussex Archaeological Collections*
SAS – Sussex Archaeological Society
SMC – Steyning Museum Collections
WSCCLS – West Sussex County Council Library Service
WSRO – West Sussex Record Office

Unacknowledged illustrations are from my own collection.

Fig. 1 Placement map, showing Chanctonbury Ring (courtesy of Mark Tibble, 'A topographical survey of Chanctonbury Ring, West Sussex: An Interpretation of the Prehistoric Landscape from the Neolithic to the Middle Iron Age', *SAC* **146**, (2008), 54, and Luke Barber, the editor of *SAC*).

Fig. 2 Janet (Pennington) with her mother Hilda Holden at Chanctonbury Ring, in the autumn of 1948.

Fig. 3 Chanctonbury Ring & Wiston pond, 1985.

Fig. 4 Sussex, from Chanctonbury Ring, 1930, 'After the water-colour drawings by Garnet R. Wolseley', in Viscountess Wolseley, *Some Sussex Byways*, (1930), Frontispiece'. I have been unable to discover who owns the copyright for Garnet Ruskin Wolseley's paintings. The Library Officer at Hove Library, where the [Viscountess] Wolseley Collection is kept, informs me that he was probably a cousin (?removed), but she does not know who owns the originals of the paintings used to illustrate Viscountess Wolseley's books or who might have an interest in the G. R. Wolseley estate. I would be grateful for any information.

Fig. 5 Chanctonbury Ring "after the storm", 1990 (SMC).

Fig. 6 Sam Carter ploughing beneath Chanctonbury, 1934 (WSRO, Garland Collection, PH 21212).

Fig. 7 'Chanctonbury Ring' by Charles Goring, 15 December 1828, copy of his poem (courtesy of Jane Goring Page).

Fig. 8 Chenkbury [*sic*] Ring from the Downs near Steyning. Sketched 1820, by W. H. Brooke (SAS).

Fig. 9 Signature of Charles Goring, 1825, part of a letter from Charles Goring to his son Charles, 27 September 1825 (courtesy of Jane Goring Page).

Fig. 10 Charles Goring, *c.* 1765, by J. S. C. Schaak (courtesy of Mr R H Goring).

Fig. 11 The suit and waistcoat worn by Charles Goring for the portrait by Schaak in Fig. 10 (courtesy of Mr R. H. Goring).

Fig. 12 King George III, Coronation Portrait, *c.* 1763. Studio of Allan Ramsay, George III © Scottish National Portrait Gallery.

Fig. 13 Wiston Park, 1928, by Garnet R. Wolseley (Viscountess Wolseley, *Sussex in the Past*, (1928), between pages 118 and 119).

Fig. 14 Datestone April 15 1747, at the south-east corner of the truncated east wing on the north side of the former courtyard of Wiston House.

Fig. 15 Wiston House, engraved by J. Greig from a drawing by T. Higham, published 1822.

Fig. 16 Lancelot ('Capability') Brown, ?1770, by Nathaniel Dance (later Sir Nathaniel Holland, Bt) © National Portrait Gallery, London.

Fig. 17 A view of Wiston, Sussex, 1826 (SAS).

Fig. 18 Chanctonbury Ring, from an old garden, *c.* 1920.

Fig. 19 Aerial photo of Chanctonbury Ring, undated (?1930s) (SAS).

Fig. 20 Dewpond at Chanctonbury Ring, looking west, 1930s (WSCCLS, PP/WSL/PC002531b).

Fig. 21Chanktonbury, 1868, by Col. Lane Fox, (*Archaeologica* **42**, (1869), from Plate VI, facing page 33).

Fig. 22 Upper Buddington Farm, Sussex Downs, *c.* 1933-1935, by John Turner (courtesy of Jill Turner).

Fig. 23 Beech tree.

Fig. 24 Norway spruce.

Fig. 25 Scots pine.

Fig. 26 Two of the largest and oldest beech stumps in Chanctonbury Ring, 2011.

Fig. 27 A broken Neolithic hammer stone, found within Chanctonbury Ring by Bob Platt, 2010 (courtesy of Bob Platt).

Fig. 28 Part of Mitchell's 1909 plan of the central Romano-Celtic temple, showing two large beech trees either side of the southernmost flint wall. (G. S. Mitchell, 'Excavations at Chanctonbury Ring, 1909', *SAC* **53**, (1910), Plate 13, opp.136, courtesy of the editor of *SAC*).

Fig. 29 Old Building discovered in Chanctonbury Ring, Wiston, Sussex' showing four beech trees on a plan of the polygonal temple (redrawn), by G. S. Mitchell, 1909 (WSRO, Wiston MS 5661).

Fig. 30 Charles Goring, 1809, by Thomas Lawrence (later Sir Thomas Lawrence) (courtesy of Mr R. H. Goring).

Fig. 31 Chanctonbury Ring, aerial view, *c.* 1965 (WSCCLS, PP/WSL/P002194)

Fig. 32 Sheep at Chanctonbury Ring, *c.* 1930s (SMC).

Fig. 33 Pip and Harry Goring with their daughters Eloise (4) and Clare (2), planting a beech sapling on Chanctonbury Ring in the autumn of 1978 (courtesy of Mr R. H. Goring & the *West Sussex Gazette*).

Fig. 34 Chanctonbury Ring from Lower Chancton, 1928, by Garnet R. Wolseley (in Viscountess Wolseley, *Sussex in the Past*, (1928), between pages 138 and 139).

Fig. 35 Ordnance Survey one-inch Old Series (First Edition), 1813, showing Upper and Lower Chancton Farms, each named as Chanctonbury F[arm].

Fig. 36 Washington, Ashington & Wiston, *c.* 1875, showing Stone Barrow/Stone Ridge at no. 7 and Wormstall (Dragon's Lair) at no. 8. (adapted from the Victoria County History (Sussex) by permission, and courtesy of the editor of *SAC* and Robin Milner-Gulland, 'The Washington Estate: New Evidence on an Ancient Boundary', *SAC* **143**, (2005), 206).

Fig. 37 Sussex, 1723, by Richard Budgen (WSRO, PM 47).

Fig. 38 An Actual Topographical Survey of the County of Sussex (southern portion), two-inches to the mile, 1780, by T. Yeakell & W. Gardner (WSRO, PM 48).

Fig. 39 Worthing and its Vicinity, 1804 (H. Smail, *The Worthing Road and Its Coaches* (1943), 12).

Fig. 40 Ordnance Survey two-inch draft map, 1806-1807 (WSRO, PM 283).

Fig. 41 Legend to map of The South Part of Wiston, *c.* 1825, by William Figg (WSRO, Wiston MS 5638).

Fig. 42 The South Part of Wiston, *c.* 1825, by William Figg, annotated by Mr John Goring (1907-1990) (Wiston MS 5638).

Fig. 43 Plan of Roman Buildings discovered at Chanctonbury Ring, 1909, by G. S. Mitchell. (see Fig. 28).

Fig. 44 Roman brooch (a bronze fibula), found during the excavation of Chanctonbury Ring, 1909 (E. Curwen & E. C. Curwen, 'Some Roman Antiquities – Wiston, Chanctonbury, and Cissbury', *SAC* **63**, *Notes & Queries* (1922), 220, courtesy of the editor of *SAC*).

Fig. 45 Cattle at Dew Pond near Chanctonbury Ring, 1930s (SMC).

Fig. 46 Cisbury [*sic*] Hill Roman Encampment near Steyning. Sketched Aug. 1820, by W. H. Brooke (SAS).

Fig. 47 Chanctonbury Ring as viewed from Cissbury Ring, undated but probably *c.* 1930 (SAS).

Fig. 48 Richard Goring, Wiston Estate Manager, with archaeologist David Rudling at Chanctonbury Ring, May 2011.

Fig. 49 Plan of Chanctonbury Ring, showing the Romano-Celtic type Temple 1 (in the centre), the Romano-British polygonal Temple 2 (to the south-west) and three Bronze Age roundbarrows to the south-east, by David Rudling (courtesy of the editor of *SAC* and David Rudling, 'Chanctonbury Ring revisited: The excavations of 1988-91', *SAC* 139 (2001), 78).

Fig. 50 Temple 1 was possibly similar to this typical Romano-Celtic temple, drawn by Guy de la Bédoyère.

Fig. 51 Temple 2 may have been something like this reconstruction of a Romano-British octagonal temple at Chelmsford (The Chelmsford temple: a reconstruction by Paul Drury, in Paul Drury, *The temple & other sites in the north-eastern sector of Caesaromagus*, CBA, **RR75**, (1988), 140, courtesy of Paul Drury and the Council for British Archaeology).

Fig. 52 Late Iron-Age/Romano-British bronze boar, found at North Farm, Washington, Sussex in 1992, length 1.2" (3.1 cm), height 0.6" (1.5 cm) (at Worthing Museum).

Fig. 53 Topographical survey of Chanctonbury Ring: the hillfort, 2008, by Mark Tibble (courtesy of the editor of *SAC* and Mark Tibble, 'A topographical survey of Chanctonbury Ring, West Sussex: An Interpretation of the Prehistoric Landscape from the Neolithic to the Middle Iron Age', *SAC* **146**, (2008), 60).

Fig. 54 Horse riders at Chanctonbury Ring, 1930s (SMC).

Fig. 55 Geoffrey the Fauconer's evidence at a Proof of Age, 1351, The National Archives, C135/113/20.

Fig. 56 'Wiston Place and Chankberry Hill', 12 January 1636, by John Dunstall snr, © Leeds Museums & Galleries. All Rights Reserved 2011.

Fig. 57 'Wiston Place and Chankberry Hill' *c.* 1646, by Wenceslaus Hollar © British Library Board, Maps*14485.(20.).

Fig. 58 The French attack on Brighton, 1514 (after British Library Cott. MS Aug. I, I, 18, courtesy of the editor of *SAC* and Frank Kitchen, 'The Ghastly War-Flame', *SAC* **124**, (1986), 180).

Fig. 59 View to Wolstonbury Hill, Newtimber Hill, the Devil's Dyke and Truleigh Hill from Chanctonbury Hill, August 2011 (courtesy of Bob Platt).

Fig. 60 Chanctonbury Ring, South Downs, 1883, by A. Elliot (WSCCLS, PP/WSL/WA000047).

Fig. 61 Chanctonbury Ring, South Downs, 1883, by A. Elliot (WSCCLS, PP/WSL/WA000046).

Fig. 62 Pamela Platt sitting under an old beech tree at Chanctonbury Ring, 1 August 2010.

Fig. 63 Wiston Park, *c.* 1880, by A. H. Hallam Murray (L. J. Jennings, *Rambles Among the Hills: In the Peak of Derbyshire and the South Downs*, (1880), facing page 187).

Fig. 64 Looking north to Surrey from Chanctonbury Hill, August 2011 (courtesy of Bob Platt).

Fig. 65 Chanctonbury Ring across the river Adur, south-west of Henfield, September 2011.

Fig. 66 Chanctonbury Ring, *c.* 1904, by F. L. Griggs (E. V. Lucas, *Highways and Byways in Sussex*, (1904), 145).

Fig. 67 Chanctonbury Ring Road, near Steyning, *c.* 1920 (SMC).

Fig. 68 Octagonal dovecote at Wiston House.

Fig. 69 The southern bank and ditch of Chanctonbury Ring, 2011.

Fig. 70 Beech roots at Chanctonbury Ring, 2011.

Fig. 71 Dr Eliot Curwen looking at the old lime tree by the Roman trackway to the north-west of Chanctonbury Ring, *c.* 1929 (SAS).

Fig. 72 Chanctonbury Ring, Wiston Pond and Wiston House, snow scene, 1947 (SMC).

Fig. 73 Chanctonbury Ring on a damp day, from the west, Summer 2010.

Fig. 74 Chanctonbury Ring, from the east, the new trees growing up within the old, Spring 2011.

Fig. 75 Janet Pennington at Chanctonbury Ring, April 2011.

Fig. 76 Janet Pennington's parents Hilda and Eric Holden excavating at the deserted medieval village of Hangleton, Hove, Sussex, *c.* 1953.

Fig. 77 Bob and Pamela Platt at Chanctonbury Ring, April 2011.

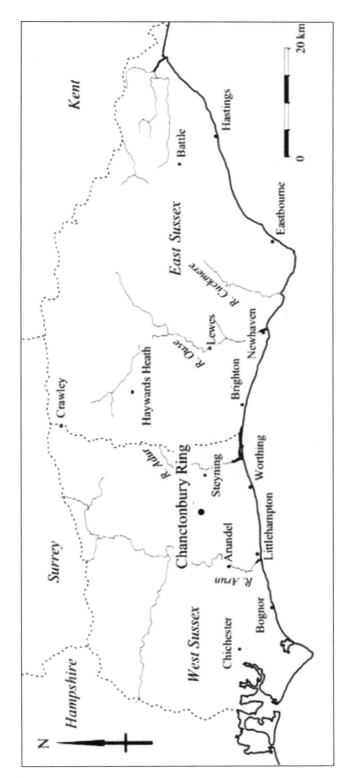

Fig. 1. Placement map, showing Chanctonbury Ring, by M. Tibble

9

Fig. 2. Janet (Pennington) with her mother, Hilda Holden, at Chanctonbury Ring in the autumn of 1948.

Foreword

*'Certain locations have the ability to retain the emotions
of generation upon generation, until they begin to exude
them like the resin that forces itself out of the veins
of a pine.'* [1] L. de Bernieres

As a child in the 1940s and 1950s I often went on outings to Chanctonbury Ring, the clump of trees planted within a prehistoric earthwork on the South Downs, to the south-west of Steyning in Sussex. On the way up, to the west of the bostal, [2] the steep track that winds to the top of the Downs on the northern escarpment, there was a special place we sometimes visited where, with our parents, my sister Pamela and I used to pick wild strawberries. Then, if we were very quiet, we could lie on the grass and look down on adders sunbathing in a chalky depression. The Ring is part of the Wiston Estate and our father, Eric Holden (1911–1989), a Sussex archaeologist, would talk about the history of the Chanctonbury site, though little organised archaeological exploration had as yet taken place there. Our mother, Hilda (1916–1995), would tell us the names of downland flowers, trees

Fig. 3. Chanctonbury Ring & Wiston Pond, 1985.

and butterflies. She also told us that walking widdershins [3] seven times around the Ring might summon the Devil, but that we should be very careful, because 'he who sups with the Devil needs for to stretch his spoon'. Despite our best (or worst) attempts, the Devil never appeared, and we were rather glad. Our mother also told us that no birds ever sang among the trees on Chanctonbury Ring, though that was probably because my sister and I were scuffling noisily in the leaf litter.

My childhood remembrances of the Ring are that it was a very special place, and I definitely had an appreciation of its almost spiritual atmosphere. It was a place to sit quietly and gaze out at the view over the northern escarpment of the Downs, at Kipling's 'wooded, dim, blue goodness of the Weald'. [4]

Fig. 4. Sussex, from Chanctonbury Ring, 1930, after Garnet R. Wolseley.

Introduction

*...when one thinks of the South Downs as a whole it is Chanctonbury
that leaps first to the inward eye. Chanctonbury, when all is said,
is the monarch of the range...It is Chanctonbury's crown of beeches
that lifts it above the other hills...its dark grove can be seen for
many miles.* [1] E. V. Lucas

Many writers, as well as E. V. Lucas, above, have commented on
the extensive views from Chanctonbury Hill. Not only Sussex,
but also, on a clear day, parts of Kent, Surrey and Hampshire are
visible '...a wonderful panorama and few in the south of England
rival it.' [2] In 1994 Bob Copper, writer, folk-singer and raconteur,
called Chanctonbury Ring '...the best-known and most affectionately
regarded landmark in Sussex...' [3]

Chanctonbury Ring is part of the South Downs National Park and a
Scheduled Ancient Monument. It is a univallate hillfort, meaning it
has one bank and ditch, and is situated on the very northern edge
of the South Downs, about 5 miles (8 km) from the coast, and 767
ft (234 m) above sea level. Most of the trees in the 'dark grove' to

Fig. 5. Chanctonbury Ring "after the storm", 1990.

Fig. 6. Sam Carter ploughing beneath Chanctonbury, 1934.

which Lucas refers were replanted in the early 1990s after their destruction by the great storm of the night of 15/16 October 1987, when an inestimable number of trees in south-eastern England were uprooted. [4] Here is not the place to write about the storm, as many others have done that, but the sight of Chanctonbury's tattered remains was heart-wrenching to most people who love Sussex and the South Downs.

The storm damage to the clump of trees covering the prehistoric hillfort on Chanctonbury Hill was very bad. The fallen trees represented 75 per cent of the total, and there were other damaged or dangerous trees that had to be removed. Proposals were put forward for a programme of replanting. 'Archaeological reasons for not replanting the trees were very evident after the storm', writes David Rudling of the Field Archaeology Unit of University College London. 'The shallow soils will inevitably lead to more fallen trees in future, and together with root damage will probably cause a threat to the interior of the Ring, and also the banks of the hillfort rampart.' [5] However, the idea of replanting the Ring met with support 'from almost every sector of the West Sussex Community' – the words of Mr R. H. Goring, then the Trustees' Manager of the Wiston Estate – and it took place after a series of archaeological excavations within the Ring by archaeologist David Rudling and his team. [6]

The following chapters tell the story of Chanctonbury Ring, the prehistoric earthwork or hillfort situated on Chanctonbury Hill, and the clump of trees planted within it. Over time the 'Ring' of the earthwork has become the 'Ring' of trees, the name remaining the same, but its meaning changing, or not, according to one's point of view. The following archaeological reports, maps, letters, literary sources and contemporary accounts reveal much of the history of Chanctonbury from prehistoric times to the present day. In particular they tell the story of the tree-planting on Chanctonbury Hill in 1760, when sixteen-year-old Charles Goring of Wiston House put a childhood dream into action.

Many inhabitants of the county of Sussex [7] know the story. In the mid-eighteenth century Sir Charles Matthew Goring (1706–1769) owned the Wiston Estate which encompasses Chanctonbury Hill. His son Charles (1744–1829) lived at the family home, Wiston House, below and to the north-east of the hill that had captured his imagination from an early age. In 1760, when he was 16 years old, he planted beech saplings within the perimeter of the ancient earth-work on its crown, supposedly carrying up bottles of water for their nourishment. He lived to the age of 85, seeing the windswept clump of trees, his 'Ring', come to maturity and he wrote a moving poem about it a year before his death. The story of Chanctonbury Ring is not quite as simple as this, but it is a fascinating story nonetheless, and one that deserves to be told.

CHAPTER 1

Charles Goring, the Ring-planter

I bow my head in homage low
To "Goring" Squire renown,
Who placed on Chancton's noble brow
This glorious living crown. [1] M. Coombe

Charles Goring of Wiston, the planter of Chanctonbury Ring in 1760, wrote the following lines in his old age:

Chanctonbury Ring

How oft around thy Ring, sweet Hill,
A Boy, I used to play,
And form my plans to plant thy top
On some auspicious day.
How oft among thy broken turf
With what delight I trod,
With what delight I placed those twigs
Beneath thy maiden sod.
And then an almost hopeless wish
Would creep within my breast,
Oh! Could I live to see thy top
In all its beauty dress'd.
That time's arrived; I've had my wish
And lived to eighty five;
I'll thank my God who gave such grace
As long as e'er I live.
Still when the morning sun in Spring
Whilst I enjoy my sight,
Shall gild thy new-clothed Beech and sides,
I'll view thee with delight.

These may not be absolutely the exact lines that he wrote. They are undoubtedly very near to the original, but possibly a few alterations have been made, spelling adjusted and punctuation added.

A poem in manuscript that belongs to the Goring family is reproduced below, followed by a transcription, though it is not in the Ring-planter's handwriting. It can be seen that the poem was not actually written when Charles was 85 years old (his 85th birthday was 29 February 1829), but when he was 84, on 15 December 1828, ten days before Christmas. In the manuscript version of the poem, after the lines 'And Lived to Eighty five' the words '8th of March next' have been added, which is rather odd, as his birthday was a week before that.

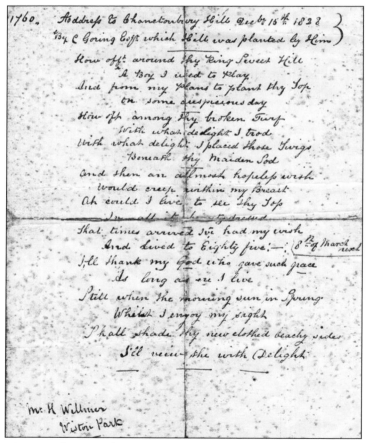

Fig. 7. 'Chanctonbury Ring', by Charles Goring, 15 December 1828.

If Charles was feeling poorly in December 1828, or thought his sight was fading, this might have spurred him on to write the poem before his birthday arrived, though he died nearly a year later, on 3 December 1829. His exclamation 'Ah' (a rather poignant word) has become 'Oh' in the frequently published version of the poem, and the Ring's 'new clothed beachy sides' has been changed to 'new-clothed Beech and sides', which does not make grammatical sense; the beech is not 'new-clothed', but the sides of the Ring are. The manuscript poem has the name 'Mr H. Willmer, Wiston Park' written on the bottom left hand side of the paper, as if a copy is to be sent to him, or else that he, Willmer, has written his name on it. The Willmer family appear in the Wiston Parish Registers from 1834–1851, the surname spelt either with one 'l' or two. Father and son, both named Henry, were gamekeepers on the estate. [2]

The manuscript poem has been transcribed, with all its eccentric spelling, and is reproduced below. Throughout his life, the Ring-planter's spelling was not consistent, and the 'Willmer version' is more likely to be nearer to the original composition:-

1760. Address to Chanctonbury Hill Dec[em]b[e]r 15th 1828
By C Goring Esq[uire] which Hill was planted by Him.

> How off[te]n around thy Ring Sweet Hill
> A Boy I used to Play
> And form my Plans to plant thy Top
> On some auspicious day
> How oft among thy broken Turf
> With what delight I trod
> With what delight I placed those Twigs
> Beneath thy Maiden Sod
> And then an allmost hopeless wish
> Would creep within my Breast
> Ah could I live to see thy Top
> In all its beauty dress'd
> That times arrived I've had my wish
> And Lived to Eighty five:- {8th of March next
> I'll thank my God who gave such grace
> As long as ere I live

Still when the morning sun in Spring
Whilst I enjoy my sight
Shall shade thy new clothed beachy sides
I'll veiw the with Delight

Mr H. Willmer
Wiston Park

Fig. 8. Chenkbury [sic] Ring from the Downs near Steyning. Sketched 1820, by W. H .Brooke.

The manuscript poem does not appear to be in the handwriting of Charles Goring. His signature, reproduced below, appears on a letter to his son Charles, dated 27 September 1825. Comparison with the 'C Goring' at the top of the manuscript poem shows differences in the way the capital letters C and G are written, as well as the terminal 'g' in Goring and there are other differences within the whole letter, though there is no doubt that he is the author of the poem.

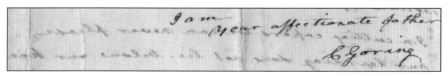

Fig. 9. Signature of Charles Goring, 1825.

In 1760, Charles Goring, then a young man of sixteen years of age and the estate owner's son, was living at Wiston House, situated below and to the north-east of Chanctonbury Hill. The portrait below shows him wearing a buff-coloured coat and breeches, holding a gun, with a spaniel at his side. J.S.C. Schaak painted in England between 1760 and 1770, so Charles can be no older than 26 in the portrait. It is more than likely that it was painted in celebration of his 21st birthday in 1765, with the sitter originally holding a woodcock, which was later replaced with a volume of Homer's works. The woodcock was clearly seen when the picture was being cleaned not long ago. [3] The Ring-planter was proficient in Latin, and when his own son Charles was at school, he encouraged him in his studies in that language. [4] The suit and waistcoat worn for the portrait are still in possession of the Goring family.

Fig. 10. Charles Goring c .1765, by J. S. C. Schaak.

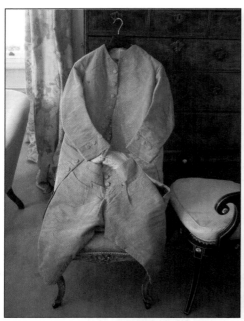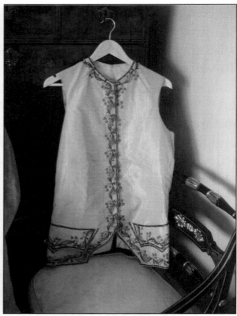

Fig. 11. The suit and waistcoat worn by Charles Goring for the portrait by Schaak in Fig. 10.

In his moving poem about the Ring, Charles indicated that when he was still a young boy he had formed his plans to plant the top of the hill with trees 'on some auspicious day'. George III was only six years older than Charles Goring himself and succeeded to the throne on 25 October 1760. The tree-planting may well have been in celebration of the new monarch, twenty two years old when he inherited the throne. George had simple personal tastes and was known to have a love of gardens. [5]

Charles Goring, the Ring-planter, was the only son of Sir Charles Matthew Goring and his second wife Elizabeth (née Fagge). [6] Elizabeth's great-grandfather had purchased the Wiston Estate in 1649, during the English Civil War. John Fagge was a young Parliamentarian soldier at the time of the purchase, whose father came from Rye in eastern Sussex. He became Sir John Fagge in 1660, pardoned by King Charles II after the Restoration, and acquiring a baronetcy. His great-grandson Robert died without a male heir, and Robert's sister Elizabeth inherited the estate. [7]

Sir Charles Goring of Highden, Washington, a neighbouring landowner from a long-established Sussex family, was a widower with three young children. In 1743, at the age of 37, he married the 40-year-old Elizabeth Fagge, whose estate was to the east of his own. [8] Certainly a marriage of land, and, one hopes, a marriage of love. There was no time to waste and their only child, Charles Goring junior, was born within a year. He had three step-siblings, twin girls and a boy, from his father's first marriage to Mary Blackborne who had died in 1739, though Charles did not seem to have been very close to them, even in later life. The twins, Mary and Elizabeth,

Fig. 12. King George III, Coronation Portrait, c .1763, studio of Allan Ramsay.© Scottish . National Portrait Gallery.

would have been about 11 years old when Charles was born, and Harry, his step-brother, about nine. Charles himself would marry three times, producing three girls with his second wife, and two sons and a daughter with his third. His youngest son John, born when he was 80, survived to inherit the estate.

Fig. 13. Wiston Park, 1928, by Garnet R. Wolseley.

As a boy, Charles no doubt went many times by foot or on horseback to the highest point of the South Downs, Chanctonbury Hill, above his home at Wiston, as his poem reveals, and looked down on the several thousand acres of the estate. [9] The house had been built by Sir Thomas Sherley in the 1570s and was in need of modernisation by the time of the Goring/Fagge marriage. It was made considerably smaller and more convenient by Charles and Elizabeth, with the removal of the eastern gatehouse range and the updating of the great hall with the addition of rococo plasterwork. The hall was made much lighter by the truncating of the wings on the east side that had previously sheltered it. A datestone records that the work was completed on 15 April 1747.

It can be surmised that the young Charles Goring had the idea of planting trees around the prehistoric earthwork on Chanctonbury Hill as a celebration of George III's accession to the throne in 1760, the 'auspicious day' of his poem, decorating the hillfort on the prominent spur of the South Downs with a fashionable clump of trees. He must have wondered about the reasons for the bank and

Fig. 14. Datestone April 15 1747, at the south-east corner of the truncated east wing on the north side of the former courtyard of Wiston House.

Fig. 15. Wiston House, engraved by J. Greig from a drawing by T. Higham, published 1822.

ditch encircling the top of the hill, and had no doubt picked up oyster shells and some of the pieces of tile and brick that littered the site, thrown up by rabbit, fox and badger activity. Scientific archaeological excavation on the South Downs was far in the future and Romano-Celtic temples in Sussex unheard of, but there must have been local tales about the earthwork that would have excited the imagination of a youngster playing around the Ring.

It would have been difficult at this time to ignore the growing influence of Lancelot 'Capability' Brown (1716-1783), landscape gardener *extraordinaire*, born in Northumberland. He became under-gardener at Stowe Park in 1740 where he was influenced by William Kent's designs. Brown married in 1744, the same year that Charles Goring, the Ring-planter, was born. He set up his own garden design practice in 1748, and moved to Hammersmith on the outskirts of London within a couple of years. His influence was soon widespread as estate owners called on him for his new and exciting plantings, as well as architectural designs for their houses and much land engineering. [10]

Fig. 16. Lancelot ('Capability') Brown, ?1770, by Nathaniel Dance, (later Sir Nathaniel Holland, Bt).© National Portrait Gallery, London.

Brown's reputation grew and he was given the nickname of 'Capability'; this was due to his habit of referring to the capabilities of the places at which he was consulted. Trees and water were perhaps the main landscape features for which he is remembered today. He utilised natural devices such as water features and strategically placed tree clumps.

Brown was working at the park of Petworth House, about 13 miles to the north-west of Wiston, in the 1750s. His first visit was in October 1751 when he surveyed the park, and he had five contracts between 1753 and 1765 from the 2nd earl of Egremont, though none of the trees he planted survived long enough to be blown down by the great storm of 1987. 'The wider park landscape was clumped, allowing a series of irregular distant views to appear between the trees.' Petworth contains all the hallmarks of his landscapes, rolling contours, the serpentine lake and the tree clumps. Brown's 1752 proposal for the park and pleasure ground at Petworth shows numerous clumps of trees. [11]

Whether Charles Goring senior and his son visited Petworth to see the landscaping there during the 1750s is unknown. [12] Whatever the

Fig. 17. A view of Wiston, Sussex, 1826.

influences, young Charles, presumably encouraged by his father, set about creating his long-lasting memorial – the clump of trees within Chanctonbury Ring. The 'Ring', as mentioned previously, should really mean the prehistoric oval-shaped earthwork surmounting the hill, but the word has come to mean the trees planted within the hillfort. For over two centuries it has been Chanctonbury Ring to everyone.

It is not known at what time of year Charles did his planting, but it is likely to have been in the autumn, after the new king had succeeded to the throne. [13] Records show that the summer of 1760 was dry and exceptionally hot, but there was an unusually mild autumn, when fruit trees, primroses and daisies bloomed. The following year was fine, with a mild winter, though a very wet autumn, which would have helped with the tree-watering. The next three years also produced much rain. [14] The geology of Chanctonbury Hill is Upper Chalk, overlaid in places with patches of Clay-with-Flints which have been encountered during archaeological excavation in the twentieth century. The soil itself is shallow.

Contrary to popular local belief, Charles did not only plant beech trees, though these were in the majority, but also spruce and Scots pines; and he did not fill the earthwork with trees. They were mainly planted around the edge and within the perimeter of the hillfort's rampart, leaving the interior open. However, there were perhaps half a dozen or more beeches planted within the Ring. If he, or his workmen, had probed the ground, they would have found the remains of the masonry from what would turn out to be two temples within the hillfort; the thick deposits of flints may have decided Charles to plant mainly around the edges. There was a beacon in the middle of the Ring in 1814 (see Chapter 4), which meant that for practical reasons it could not have been thickly planted then. The wars with France from 1793 to 1802, then again from 1803 to 1815 would have precluded obscuring an important beacon site.

The local story that has echoed down some decades relates that Charles walked (or perhaps rode) up to the site every day to water the trees, apparently carrying bottles of water. If one thinks about the logistics, he would have needed very many bottles, and very many journeys. The watering would no doubt have been done by the estate workers, using horse-drawn water carts, though perhaps supervised by him. It is unlikely that they would have come up the steep northern escarpment with water, as there are other water sources within half a mile, to the south of the Ring. Three nearby dewponds were apparently not made until the 1870s and these, and other water sources, will be discussed below.

Fig. 18. Chanctonbury Ring, from an old garden c. 1920.

John Butcher, a farmworker on the Wiston Estate who died in 1967 in his eighties (and who is mentioned in Chapter 3), related that his grandfather 'Mas' Butcher of Locks Farm, under the Ring, found some Roman coins '...when planting the outside ring of trees for Mr Goring'. However, it does not seem possible that his grandfather could have worked for the Ring-planter in 1760, though it might have been an earlier forbear, unless he was talking about a replanting in the nineteenth century or perhaps in 1909. [15]

The photograph on the following page (Fig. 19), with north to the left, shows a dewpond to the south-east of the Ring, on the ridge of the South Downs. It also shows the tree-planting filling the earthwork. The earlier, outer ring of trees can just be distinguished as slightly lighter than the inner fill which would have been about

20 or 30 years old. [16] Dewponds, formerly called rain ponds, were known in prehistoric times in various parts of the country, but they had a revival in the nineteenth and twentieth centuries with the intensive use of the Downs for sheep grazing, when the word dewpond was applied to them, overtaking the word rain pond. The Chanctonbury downland had three dewponds, though Sussex archaeologist Dr E. C. Curwen only noted two *c.* 1928, recording one to the west of the Ring on the 6-inch Ordnance Survey map of the area as 'A dewpond made by Rev. J. Goring 1874'. The south-eastern one he records as 'A dewpond made a few years after that'. [17]

The Society of Sussex Downsmen (now the South Downs Society) restored one of the western ponds in 1971, and reported that it was 'built by Mr Herbert Floute, an old tenant of the Rev. J. Goring. Mr Floute, a lime-burner and farmer, himself "puddled" the pond with clay and flints'. [18] A '...pocket of clay was found which was used for puddling...' writes a correspondent to the *Sussex County Magazine* in 1942. [19] The name Floute seems to be a mis-spelling of Floate. The

Fig. 19. Aerial photo of Chanctonbury Ring, undated (?1930s).

Fig. 20. Dewpond at Chanctonbury Ring (looking west), 1930s.

Census Return for Washington village in 1881 shows Herbert James Floate, aged 30, living at Ebbourn House near the lime kilns there. It is marked as Elbourne House on modern O/S maps. Floate is described as a lime merchant, and the lime kilns were to the eastern side of what is now the Old London Road at Washington, to the south of the *Frankland Arms* public house. Floate's sister Alice, aged 27, acted as his housekeeper. The Revd. John Goring (1824–1905), the Ring-planter's youngest and only surviving son, was the owner of the Wiston Estate at that time.

The work on the dewponds in the 1870s may have been repair work to much older ponds, though this is refuted by a correspondent to the *Sussex County Magazine* (see below). Dewponds fill naturally with rainwater, and the idea that they are replenished by mist and dew is not now supported. Had they been in existence in 1760, the ponds would have been a useful source of water for the young Charles Goring. However, this seems unlikely from evidence provided by correspondents to the *Sussex County Magazine*, below. He may have arranged for the young trees to have flints piled up around their bases, which would have attracted moisture from the downland mists and kept them damp, as recommended by J.W. Worledge a century before. [20]

Mr G. Ralph Hide (or Hyde) of Findon wrote to the *Sussex County Magazine* in October 1941, saying that the ponds were due to the thoughtfulness of the Revd John Goring of Wiston House. Mr Hide had a herd of 'Scotch cattle' [21] on that part of the downland and states that the Revd John Goring made three dewponds. One was to the south-east of the Ring; the other two were to the west of the Ring, 100 yards from each other, though 'Hampton's Pond' was hidden in the gorse by 1941. These two were made for Mr Herbert Floute [sic], a farmer and lime burner, tenant of the estate and an intimate friend of Mr Hide's, and also for tenant Mr George Hampton of North End Farm, Findon. The Revd John apparently said 'You must puddle the pond, Flouty', which he did with clay and flints, the clay occurring naturally on site. He added one and a half loads from a water cart after the puddling was done. Mr Hide mentioned that no straw was used in the making of any of the ponds. [22]

This letter was followed up in February 1942 by another correspondent. Mr Edward Martin of Patcham (who spells Hide as Hyde, and Floute as Floate) had been in correspondence with 85 year old Mr Hyde, who told him there were no dewponds on the hill when he was a boy, mentioning that his own father, who died in 1887, had never seen any ponds on Chanctonbury before the new ones made in 1874. This Mr Martin may have been the geologist Edward Martin, who met up with Mr Hyde 20 years earlier, and was the author of a paper on dewponds that he read to the Royal Society. [23]

Colonel Lane Fox (later General Pitt-Rivers) had made a general study of the archaeology of the South Downs in the mid-nineteenth century, and read his paper about Sussex hillforts to the Society of Antiquaries in 1868. He had opened some barrows (burial mounds) near the Ring but did not find anything. He states that there was a depression that may have been some sort of pond to the south of Chanctonbury Ring, taking in the drainage from two coombes. [24]

Archaeologists Dr Eliot Curwen and his son Dr Eliot Cecil Curwen mention an old well in Well Bottom (TQ 1345 1150, a deep coombe south-west of Chanctonbury Ring), in their article on covered ways on the Sussex Downs, presuming that this is what Lane Fox meant by 'Ancient Well' on his map (see Fig. 21). [25] However, the latter's map almost certainly refers to Upper Buddington Farm pond, more or less due south of the Ring, and not Well Bottom. A pond is still shown near the former farmhouse site on the Ordnance Survey six-inch map (TQ1395 1110) in 1958. The well from which Well Bottom presumably took its name does not seem to have been in the Bottom itself, but curiously on much higher ground *c.* 750 yards (0.68 km) to the south-west, in Findon parish (TQ 1265 1130). It is marked on Ordnance Survey maps until the mid-twentieth century, with a Well House noted in 1879. It is noteworthy that the parish boundaries of Wiston, Washington and Findon all meet at Well Bottom, and Robin Milner-Gulland (see p. 53) presumes that all three needed a share in a downland well hereabouts. [26]

Exploration reveals no well in Well Bottom, and the site of the well on the ridge to the south-west shown on earlier maps is now covered in scrub and trees, though there are big water tanks nearby. [27] The 'Ancient Well' shown in Fig. 21 below, to the south of the Ring, is almost certainly the pond or the well (there is one of each) at the now demolished Upper Buddington farmhouse.

A visit to the site of Upper Buddington Farm (demolished during World War II), just over half a mile (1 km) due south of Chanctonbury Ring (TQ 1395 1110), reveals that across the track to the north-east of the farmhouse site there is a depression that must have been the

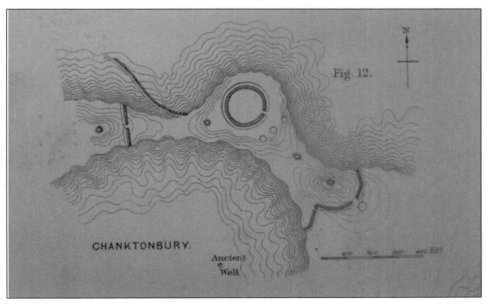

Fig. 21. Chanktonbury, 1868, by Col. Lane Fox.

pond. Though empty of water in the driest summer for many years (August 2010), it would normally receive any water arriving there from two steep slopes above. Tree cover and undergrowth make it difficult to see exactly how deep the pond would have been; it is marked on Ordnance Survey maps until the mid-twentieth century. [28] It would have been much easier and quicker to cart water from here to Chanctonbury Ring than from the bottom of the north side of the downland escarpment, or from Washington to the west. There is also a well near the former farmhouse site but it was too overgrown to explore this area.

Whatever the truth about the watering of the young trees, they were growing strongly enough a quarter of a century later when, in 1786, Charles Goring, now 42, and owner of the estate, entered into a boundary dispute with a neighbour, Revd Roger Clough Esq. of Warminghurst, Sussex. Clough owned the manor of Chancton, a landholding that included Upper and Lower Chancton Farms (see Fig. 35), and which abutted Wiston manorial holdings. Draft letters by Charles, with Clough's replies, survive to show that the two men, who obviously knew each other fairly well, were jostling with some

Fig. 22. Upper Buddington Farm, Sussex Downs, c. 1933-35, by John Turner.

literary force for land ownership, rights and boundary accuracy. The earliest letter to survive, a draft by Charles Goring, addressed to Roger Clough Esq. of Warminghurst is set out below, spelling and grammar unchanged:

> *Sir, My servant informs me that a great part of my*
> *Down with the Ring on Chankburry was yesterday trod*
> *in as Part of your Manor & that the Turf was dug up in*
> *several places as bound marks, & that some other Lands*
> *in the Parish of Wiston were likewise trod in which I*
> *have uninterruptedly enjoyed as part of the Manor of*
> *Wiston for which I have a grant with right of free*
> *Chace, under the G[rea]t seal of Edward the third confir-*
> *m'd afterwards by Eliz[abeth] & Charles 2 & James 1st.*
> *I am extremely sorry any matter shoud arise to cause a*
> *Dispute between Families who formerly livd in friend-*
> *ship & good neighbourhood, but the Right in question*
> *w[hi]ch is of great consequence to my estate but little to*
> *yours [several lines deleted here]...I on my part must be*
> *defended as I have not the least doubt about it, & so I*
> *sincerely hope you will upon fuller information order the*
> *Proceedings of yesterday to be undone.*
> *Mrs. G joins in Comp[limen]ts to the Ladies. I am etc.*
> *C. G. Sept 28 1786.* [29]

Clough replied on 30 September, firmly staking his claim, saying he has written evidence:

> *...long since the Reign of Chas I that the Down, Holt,*
> *Coppice, & Owlscroft, trod in the 18th Inst. were*
> *certainly part of Chancton...Altho' the Down etc. were*
> *sold off from Chancton Farm...the Manorial Rights,*
> *I conceive, could not possibly be separated from the*
> *Manor. As to the Lands trod in in the Parish of Wiston*
> *they have ever been, & still are held of the Manor of*
> *Chancton.*

He suggested that they meet with his attorney to discuss the matter. [30] Charles's draft reply indicates in that case he would like to meet in town and would have his own solicitor present '...*as many inconveniences may arise when a Gentleman has to treat with a professional man'.* Charles spells 'Chankbury' in this letter with only one 'r', going into further details about shooting rights and trespass by Clough's gamekeeper, ending his letter by saying:

> *As I have been thus open and candid with you I doubt*
> *not but you will in like manner explain to me the*
> *Grounds of your claim upon my Freehold Lands...Mrs*
> *G joins in Com[plimen]ts to the Ladies.*
>
> *I am, yr etc. Sept 30 1786* [31]

One hopes that Mrs. Goring was sincere in joining her husband with compliments to the Clough ladies. The last surviving letter (from Clough) dated 3 October 1786, is torn and fragmentary:

> *...with regard to Chankbury, I can add but little to what*
> *I have already said, being still of the opinion that the*
> *manorial Rights thereto, could not be separated from the*
> *Manor...* [32]

He suggests they meet at Steyning on 19 or 20 October. Charles Goring has written a draft letter on part of Clough's letter, dated 14 October 1786, interestingly stating that

> *I rec[eive]d a letter from my solicitor this day and I will*
> *be fair to tell you it is in favor of your Claim on*
> *Chankbury in some sort, but it is not so...*

There, irritatingly, the letter ends, as it has been torn. The details of what followed are unknown, though Charles seems to have kept the rights to Chanctonbury, with Clough keeping those to Chancton manor. In 1805, the year of the Battle of Trafalgar, Clough sold the manor to the duke of Norfolk, and the lands eventually came back to the Goring family in the nineteenth century. [33]

The survey of the estate undertaken by William Figg some years later, *c.* 1825, hopefully clarified the situation. The Ring-planter was an elderly gentleman by then, in his early eighties. With a second son, John, born in 1824 (his first son, Charles, was to die in 1849 at the age of 32, when John inherited the estate), Charles was no doubt feeling the weight of his years. With a third and much younger wife, Mary, he probably wished to have a new survey done so that she would have no problems over land disputes after his death. He died in December 1829, having lived through stirring times. During his lifetime the American colonies became independent (1776), King Louis XVI of France was guillotined (1793) the French Revolutionary and Napoleonic Wars took place, with the Battle of Trafalgar (1805) and the Battle of Waterloo (1815). He would no doubt have felt much sorrow at the final long illness of George III, who died in 1820 after a decade of misery. [34] He would also have been interested in the industrial improvements that were taking place, revolutionising agriculture. The Ring-planter was awarded a prize for his essay on the conversion of grass to arable, which was published by the Board of Agriculture in 1802. [35] The recording of farmland has always been of great importance to landowners, and Charles would have been aware of the Ordnance Survey mapping campaigns (see Chapter 3).

Figg's twenty-eight maps of the Wiston Estate lands, surveyed c. 1825, are beautifully drawn, with all the field names and farms listed, Chanctonbury Ring amongst them. The maps have been annotated by Mr John Goring (1907–1990), the Ring-planter's great-grandson (see Fig. 42), who took a great interest in the history of his estate. He deposited many thousands of documents from his estate archive, dating from the thirteenth to the twentieth centuries, at the West Sussex Record Office, Chichester, in the 1960s, and again in the 1970s. [36] Mr J. M. L. Booker, who catalogued the documents comprising Volume 1 of the Wiston Archives by 1968, wrote in his Introduction:

> All students of local history will join with the County Record Office in thanking Mr John Goring for his generosity in the deposit of this collection. It is only through acts of this nature that the full picture of English history at a regional level can be appreciated and students, in the anonymity of the public research room, may perhaps forget the kindness of the private depositor. [37]

CHAPTER 2

The Trees of Chanctonbury Ring

*'...each beautifully arched by nature in conformity with
the smooth rounded hilltops, the outer trees being stunted
by the wind and the inner ones rising above them
in the shelter, seeking light.'* [1] P. Brandon

The European beech – *Fagus sylvatica* – is drought resistant. It is one of the largest British trees, and grows especially well on chalky or sandy soils. In England it may grow to over 100 feet in height, the same in its spread of branches. Owing to the capacity of its root system for assisting in the circulation of air throughout the soil, and by the amount of potash in the leaves, beech trees conserve the productive capacity of the soil better than any other kind of tree, and improve the growth of other trees when planted with them. They would thus have helped the Ring-planter's other tree varieties, the spruce and Scots pine, to thrive.

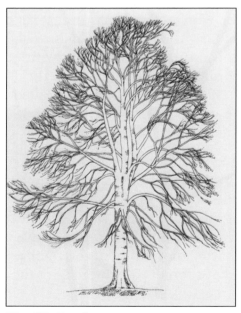

Fig. 23. Beech tree.

Beech trees prefer full sun and grow fairly slowly, living up to 350 years in the most favourable conditions, though on an exposed site like Chanctonbury Hill, with the prevailing south-westerly winds, one would expect a shorter life-span. The great storm of 1987 that hit south-eastern England on the night of 15/16 October ravaged the Ring. Many trees would have been just over 225 years of age. Mr John Goring, the owner of the Wiston Estate, said that the oldest trees had more or less come to the end of their natural lifespan by 1987, and that the storm had finished them off. [2]

The evergreen Norway spruce – *Picea abies* – now the traditional Christmas tree, was introduced from Europe or Scandinavia *c*. AD 1500 and increasingly planted in this country from the seventeenth century. It is sensitive to exposure, but thrives well under frosty conditions. Its evergreen properties may have appealed to the young Charles Goring.

Fig. 24. Norway spruce.

The Scots pine – *Pinus sylvestris* – is very hardy, the only native conifer grown for timber production. It grows well in the warmer and drier districts of south-eastern England, where it has proved very successful as a shelterbelt tree. It is also an evergreen, and perhaps Charles chose it for both these reasons.

Fig. 25. Scots pine.

An exploratory visit to the Ring to look at the trees on 1 August 2010 showed that none of the very old trees are still growing; however, there are many stumps and root balls of the 1760 beech plantings around the circumference of the earthwork, some actually on it, some within it and a few outside it. On a visit to the Ring on 11 April 2011, approximately 160 large old stumps and root balls were counted, about 34 of these outside the bank and ditch, and the rest scattered around the interior. Some were of such a size that they must be remnants of the 1760 planting. Two of the largest stumps are probably those noted in 1909 as 'large beech trees' in Fig. 28.

The majority of the growing trees are beech. Some of these, and the sycamores, look to be about 100 years old. There are also some ash

Fig. 26. Two of the largest and oldest beech stumps in Chanctonbury Ring, 2011.

trees. There is no sign of spruce or Scots pine, though some small pinecones were seen. Harry Goring remembers from some years ago at least three Scots pines situated at the south-east corner of the Ring, small and bent, used as nurse trees from an earlier planting.[3] Flints and Roman tile are widely distributed and seem to have been very much disturbed by the later plantings, as well as by rabbit, fox and badger diggings. Oyster shells can be seen, and a piece of broken marble was found in 2010, part of a Neolithic hammer stone. [4]

Fig. 27. A broken Neolithic hammer stone, found within Chanctonbury Ring, 2010.

George Mitchell, the estate manager, undertook the first archaeological excavation at Chanctonbury Ring in 1909, described in Chapter 3. He was not a trained archaeologist, but published his report in the *Sussex Archaeological Collections* the following year, beginning with the following lines:

> Probably no point upon the Southdowns is more
> widely known than is Chanctonbury, not only
> because it forms one of the most commanding
> heights in the County of Sussex...but because its bold
> clump of trees renders it so easily distinguishable at
> great distances from the north, east and west. [5]

He continues that 'tradition states' that when only a schoolboy, Charles Goring, 'having planted some beech seedlings there' afterwards carried up bottles of water and nourished them. 'In later life he still continued to plant...' though whether this was in the Ring or elsewhere is not stated. The Ring-planter was a great arboriculturist. [6] Mitchell writes that Charles's knowledge and love of trees was remembered by the Lawrence portrait in Fig. 30 below.

The estate manager notes that by 1909, the original beech, spruce and Scots pine trees, which had attained a considerable size, '...have begun to die out, and a certain amount of replacement has become necessary, the evergreen oak, sycamore and Scots fir [Scots pine] being chiefly used for that purpose.' It is not clear when these latter trees were planted. The Holm or Evergreen oak – *Quercus ilex* – Britain's only common evergreen oak, was introduced during the sixteenth century from the Mediterranean. It is a moderate sized tree with a broad, rounded, dense crown. The leaves are very different from the English oak – *Quercus robur* – by long tradition the deciduous national tree of England. The Holm oak, whose leaves are almost oval and never lobed, is a useful screen and gives shelter from sun and wind. It is particularly good by the sea because it gives shade and shelter and resists the ill-effects of salt laden winds. It would have been a useful and attractive tree to plant on Chanctonbury, and there is a brief mention of it in a newspaper cutting dating from the autumn of 1978, which reveals that 'The Ring has consisted of beech, ash and larch trees, but there are few larches now. Mr John Davey [the Head Forester] said there was a chestnut as well as Holm oak, sycamore and Scots pine still to be seen'. [7] There are two fine specimens of Holm oak to the north of Wiston House, which were possibly planted 150 or more years ago, and another one south-east of the churchyard wall.

Mitchell also states that 'The central portion of the area enclosed by "the Ring" has not hitherto been planted, and with the intention of filling this also with trees, trenching operations were carried out during the summer of 1909'. This is a strange statement, when he clearly shows six beech trees on his plans of the interior of the earthwork, two of which he calls 'Large' and which must have been there for many years, perhaps from 1760 (see Figs. 26, 28 & 29). There were other old trees scattered about in the centre of the Ring, judging by the large root balls seen in 2010 and 2011. Perhaps he just meant it was not filled with trees. The Ring-planter's grandson Charles (son of the Revd John Goring who died in 1905) born 12 September 1862 and aged 47 when Mitchell excavated, would no doubt have visited during the digging and discussed the history of the ring-planting by his own grandfather with his estate manager. It is unlikely that the absence of trees (apart from the six noted on his plan) within the Ring itself would have been invented by Mitchell in his archaeological report, a copy of which would also have gone to Charles Goring, the owner of the Ring, as well as for publication in *Sussex Archaeological Collections*.

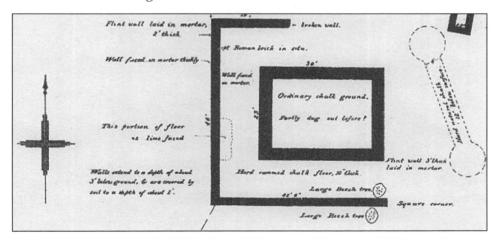

Fig. 28. Part of Mitchell's 1909 plan of the central Romano-Celtic temple showing two large beech trees either side of the southernmost flint wall. The dotted line (lower left) leads to the polygonal temple shown in Fig. 29.

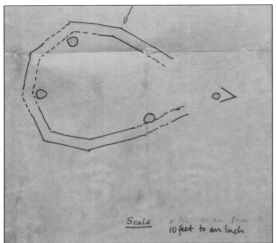

Fig. 29. 'Old Building discovered in Chanctonbury Ring, Wiston, Sussex', showing four beech trees on a plan [redrawn] of the polygonal temple 62ft to the south-west of the central temple, by G. S. Mitchell, 1909.

Fig. 30. Charles Goring, 1809, by Thomas Lawrence (later Sir Thomas Lawrence).

The portrait (Fig. 30) on the facing page shows the Ring-planter, aged 65, holding an oak sapling. The Goring family has always felt that it should have been a beech sapling, but it may be that the artist persuaded the sitter that the oak, the traditional 'national tree' of England, was more representative of an English country gentleman than a beech. [8]

The contour of Chanctonbury Ring in Fig. 31 shows how the prevailing south-westerly winds shaped the trees as they grew. However, photographs taken of the Ring only 20 or 30 years after the 1909 plantings would indicate that the trees in the centre must have grown fairly quickly within the shelter of the outer ring, though light can be seen through them.

Sussex author and historian Dr Peter Brandon states that Hadrian Allcroft 'a prodigious archaeologist' (though Allcroft seems to have got a lot of facts wrong) wrote in 1908 of the 'round clump of beeches filling Chanctonbury Ring', though according to Mitchell the centre was not planted. Allcroft said that 'not even an archaeologist would bear him [Charles Goring] ill will for that he planted his trees upon a 'camp' and amidst broken remains of a Roman building', though that statement might be queried by archaeologists a century later. [9]

Fig. 31. Chanctonbury Ring, aerial view, c. 1965.

The sycamore – *Acer pseudoplatanus* – is the other tree referred to by Mitchell in 1909. It was brought from France in medieval times and seeds profusely. It is tall and attractive, with masses of matt green foliage and is an excellent shelterbelt tree. The additional tree-plantings, whenever and however often they took place, unsurprisingly needed these shelterbelt trees to protect the ageing beeches planted in 1760.

The Forester's Book for the Wiston Estate shows that in 1931 the trees were 'dwarfed by wind and have no commercial value but...are healthy'. The entry continues 'Trees have been planted at later dates to replace deaths. 1935. A quantity of dead wood was removed for 'Jubilee' bonfire'. [10] This, of course, would have been in celebration of the Silver Jubilee of King George V.

Mr Philip Gosse, who lived on the Wiston Estate and is mentioned in Chapter 5, gave an alarming report of the condition of the trees in the Jubilee year of 1935. The editor of the *Sussex County Magazine* reported in December of that year that Gosse had said the Ring was getting very thin. 'A number of the beeches have fallen and the bad weather has been affecting them. A big hole has appeared in the ground, and I fear that gradually the trees will be condemned.' The

Fig. 32. Sheep at Chanctonbury Ring, c. 1930s.

owner, Mr John Goring, grandson of the Revd John, and great-grandson of the Ring-planter, had said he would '...make good the gaps by planting thirty or forty new trees'. The editorial ended with the words 'Chanctonbury without its beeches would be unthinkable'. The trees were apparently counted at this time, and 230 were noted, though how many of each species is not recorded. [11]

However, the editor got a sharp rebuff from Mr Edward Shoosmith, who wrote in January 1936 of the '...utter uselessness of replanting young trees under or even within several yards of old timber.' He explained that the young trees, especially on the north side of the Ring, would invariably '...draw away from their towering hosts and grow up stunted and ill-shapen'. He said that the only hope of pre-serving well-grown successors of the trees would be to form '...a completely new plantation on the outside of the present one and a rather considerable distance away'. [12] This was not done, however, though archaeologists might have wished it so.

The editor '& Friends' wrote that 'from time to time the clump has been renewed, the last planting having been at the beginning of the present century...it is Mr Goring's intention during the next few years to plant a further 30 or 40 beech and ash trees to secure the perpetuation of the group...' [13]

Charles Grigg of Steyning published some local memories in 1967, which included a paragraph on Chanctonbury Ring. He said that the trees there were always well cared for and that in 1959 the owner of the Wiston Estate, John Goring, '...had a further 200 trees of beech, sycamore and ash planted to replace the ravages of time.' [14] However, he may have misremembered the date, as Harry Goring states that his father planted 200-300 beeches within the Ring in 1961. A grant was offered for the trees at this time by West Sussex County Council (WSCC), but John Goring turned it down. [15]

Various stories about the number of trees at Chanctonbury Ring have circulated locally in the twentieth century. Dr Jacqueline Simpson is a Sussex folklore expert, and c. 1938 her father told her that nobody could count the trees properly, because there is some sort of spell on them. Other people believe that 365 trees were originally planted, one for each day of the year, though there is absolutely no proof of this. Mr John Goring stated in the 1960s that the trees were last counted in 1935, and that there were then 230. Some have since fallen, and others have been planted, but there is no attempt by the Wiston Estate to keep to a specific number. [16] When archaeologist Owen Bedwin excavated at Chanctonbury Ring in 1977 (see Chapter 3) he noted that the clump of trees was mostly beech, with the occasional sycamore. Rudling mentions the uncertainty of whether or not the centre of the Ring was planted in 1909 or before. [17]

A year after Bedwin's excavation, 840 three-to-four-year old trees were planted by the Estate foresters in 1978. A WSCC grant helped to pay for 600 beech, 170 Scots pine and 70 Lawson cypress saplings, planted five feet apart. Harry Goring explains that 'the object of the softwood was to act as a 'nurse' to the beech in the form of protection of the elements and as a competitor for light. The beech grows up, straight and tall, rather than out like a bush. The nurse crop is thinned over the years and eventually removed altogether'. [18]

Fig. 33. Pip and Harry Goring with their daughters Eloise (4) and Clare (2), planting a beech sapling on Chanctonbury Ring in the autumn of 1978.

In 1988, as mentioned in the Introduction, Harry Goring stated that the idea of replanting the Ring after the great storm of 1987 met with support 'from almost every sector of the West Sussex Community', and indeed this was so. Letters to the *West Sussex Gazette* from Dr Peter Brandon, and the author amongst others, reveal the strength of feeling for replanting the trees on this prominent landscape feature. English Heritage felt it should be flexible and responsive, and WSCC was supportive. Before the replanting went ahead, a fresh archaeological analysis of the site was organised. With the full support of the Goring family, the project to undertake assessment excavations to investigate some of the exposure of Roman material resulting from the storm went ahead, and this is described in Chapter 3. [19]

In 1990 four hundred trees were planted, mainly beech, to fill up the gaps caused by the great storm. Harry Goring had applied to English Heritage for permission to plant in May 1989, but the approval did not come through until February 1990. In effect this was a blessing in disguise:

> ...because in the severe gale of January 1990, a
> further 31 trees blew down, creating more gaps and
> more light. If the new planting had taken place in
> the autumn of 1989, the young trees would have
> been severely damaged. [20]

Brandon feels that '...many imitative coronals on the Downs...' were planted after Charles Goring's example of 1760, '...each beautifully arched by nature in conformity with the smooth rounded hilltops, the outer trees being stunted by the wind and the inner ones rising above them in the shelter, seeking light. [21] He also worried in 1998 that '...until recently the lower slopes of Chanctonbury Ring were completely free of scrub which now grows thickly at the base of the Ring and does not set it off so dramatically.' [22] This is still the case, but there are no plans to clear trees and scrub from the northern escarpment below the Ring. [23]

Brandon goes on to say that young Charles Goring, the Ring-planter, 'gave a new significance to Chanctonbury as one of the "Good Places" that help us to feel more at home in our world, and with

God, as Mervyn Stockwood, past bishop of Southwark, has revealed in his recent autobiography, appropriately entitled *The Ring*.' [24]

So, to conclude the arboreal story to date, it can be seen that after that first momentous planting in 1760, the trees, having a finite life, have needed to be replenished and nurtured for the last quarter of a millennium. In the twentieth century there are at least five documented accounts of new and replacement tree-plantings at the Ring, and perhaps it will continue for another quarter of a millennium, unless archaeological opinion dictates otherwise. However, Chanctonbury Ring has taken hold of the regional imagination. In a large part it represents the county of Sussex, and provides a familiar, reassuring landmark to local inhabitants and returning travellers alike.

CHAPTER 3

The Archaeology and Early History of Chanctonbury and the Ring

'There is no reason why the interpretation of past human communities should be any less complicated than our less than complete understanding of contemporary society'. [1] M. Tibble

Chanctonbury was not called by this name until the late-eighteenth century – it had for centuries been something like 'Changebury' or 'Chankbury'. Land owner and Ring-planter Charles Goring wrote '...my Down with the Ring on Chankburry...' when disputing the boundaries of Chancton manor in 1786. [2]

Fig. 34. Chanctonbury Ring from Lower Chancton, 1928, by Garnet R. Wolseley.

The manor, or landholding, of Chancton (part of the Wiston Estate) was known before 1066 and in later times was in two parts, the larger to the north of the parish of Washington and the smaller to the south, though it took in parts of Wiston, Washington and Ashington parishes.

The manor was sold to Sir Thomas Sherley of Wiston House in 1592, passing through various owners to the Revd Roger Clough. The latter married into the Butler family of Warminghurst in Sussex and eventually sold the whole of Chancton manor to the duke of Norfolk in 1805, less than a decade after the boundary dispute with Charles Goring which is discussed in Chapter 1. The manor apparently did not include Chanctonbury Ring. Upper and Lower Chancton Farms survive today on the Wiston Estate, and Lower Chancton was probably the site of the original manor house, now represented by the seventeenth century timber-framed building, illustrated in Fig. 34. Dr Tim Hudson, the editor of the *Victoria County History* for this part of Sussex, feels that Chanctonbury Ring – the

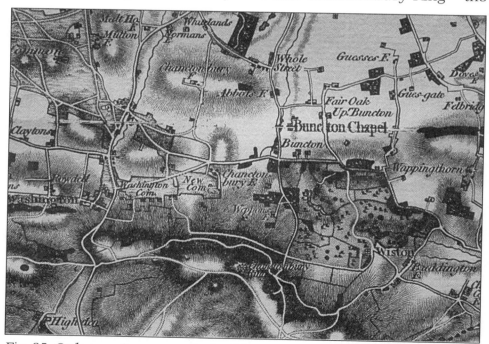

Fig. 35. Ordnance Survey one-inch Old Series (First Edition) 1813 map, showing Upper and Lower Chancton Farms, each named as Chanctonbury F[arm]. Chanctonbury Ring is clearly marked.

hillfort – had never been included in either of the adjoining parishes of Wiston or Washington, though the parish boundaries now bisect the prehistoric earthwork. He writes that across Chanctonbury Hill the Wiston–Washington boundary was undefined in the past. Boundary marks in that area were mentioned in 1530, but by the end of the eighteenth century the boundary between the manors of Chancton and Wiston, and their parishes, was uncertain. [3]

However, unlike Hudson, Robin Milner-Gulland thinks that the Washington/Wiston boundary may have passed across the hillfort of Chanctonbury more than a thousand years ago. He has used two Anglo-Saxon charters for Washington (whose parish boundary adjoins that of Wiston), dated AD 947 and AD 963, to explore the boundaries and the landscape. He thinks it possible that the names 'Stone Barrow' from the AD 947 charter and 'Stone Ridge' from AD 963 could indicate the flint-built temples within the hillfort, which are discussed below (see Fig. 36). [4]

Fig. 36. Washington, Ashington and Wiston, c. 1875, showing Stone Barrow/Stone Ridge at no. 7 and Wormstall (Dragon's Lair) at no. 8, by R. Milner-Gulland.

Fig. 37 shows the earliest road map of Sussex, published in 1723. The words 'Chankbury hill' can be seen to the top right of the 'O' of 'STORRINGTON', with the oval representation of the hillfort just to the left of the top of the first 'R'. Cissbury hill can be seen to the south. The long 's' was used in printing at this time, so what appears to be 'Wilton' (circled), between the tops of the two R's of Storrington, is actually 'Wiston', showing the position of the house.

The forerunner of the early Ordnance Survey maps is the Yeakell and Gardner Sussex series of 1778-83. Charles Lennox, the third duke of Richmond, employed the two cartographers to make plans of his Goodwood Estate. He was Master-General of the Ordnance between 1782 and 1795. Only four sheets of the proposed eight were engraved, but Sheet 2, published in 1780, includes the Wiston Estate and Chanctonbury Hill, though the latter is spelt 'Chancbury', as shown in Fig. 38. The Ring is depicted but not named. [5]

The Ordnance Survey was founded in 1791 and the first director, appointed by Charles Lennox in July of that year, was Major

Fig. 37. Sussex, 1723, by Richard Budgen.

Edward Williams, with Lieutenant William Mudge as his deputy. Isaac Dalby had been appointed assistant to the Ordnance Survey a few weeks before. The three men were to undertake the organisation of 'the Trigonometrical Survey' or 'The duke of Richmond's Survey' as it was sometimes called, a national survey of the country. The French Revolution was in full swing, and military commanders in England needed an accurate map of the south coast as soon as possible, as a French invasion was feared. The whole story of the Survey can be read in Rachel Hewitt's *Map of a Nation* (2010), where she explains that Mudge, Williams and Dalby spent much of 1793 in Sussex. Their plan of the 'Principal Triangles' measured between 1791 and 1794 clearly shows 'Chanctonbury Ring' with eight triangulations drawn from that point. This is the earliest reference discovered for the spelling of the name 'Chanctonbury'. [6]

Fig. 38. An Actual Topographical Survey of the County of Sussex (southern portion), two-inches to the mile, 1780, by T. Yeakell & W. Gardner.

However, a map of 'Worthing and its Vicinity', published in 1804, depicts 'Chankbury Hill' to the west of Steyning, in Fig. 39. [7] It was still being called Chankbury locally in 1814, and a visitor, having a picnic on the hill with a group of friends in 1818, wrote 'Chanckbury' in his description (see Chapter 5). [8] A draft Ordnance Survey map of 1806–1807 (see Fig. 40) uses the words 'Chanctonbury Ring', as does the 1813 version in Fig. 35, presumably having taken this spelling from the 'Principal Triangles' plan. [9]

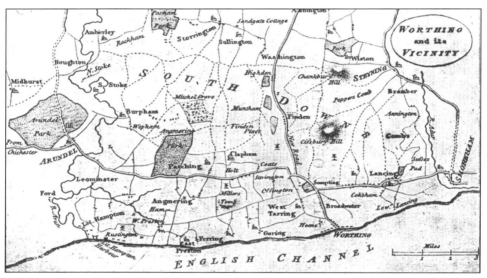

Fig. 39. Worthing and its Vicinity, 1804.

The 'new' spelling of Chanctonbury also appears on the legend of a map of the south part of Wiston, surveyed by William Figg of Lewes *c.* 1825. This was probably the fourth William Figg of this family (1799-1866), a founder member of the Sussex Archaeological Society. [10] Figg would no doubt have been up to date with the Ordnance Survey mapping of the county, as well as the Trigonometrical Survey, and presumably copied their spelling, which he may have pointed out to Charles Goring. The name written as 'Chanctonbury Ring' can be seen at no. 6 in Fig. 41. Hudson feels that the change of name was the result of antiquarianism. [11] The Ring-planter's son, the Revd John Goring, still writes 'Chankbury' in the 1860s. [12]

So it seems that the name change from something like Chankbury to Chanctonbury, the spelling that we know today, was first documented *c.* 1794, when the 'Principal Triangles' plan was produced, but the old spelling and pronunciation lingered on locally for many years.

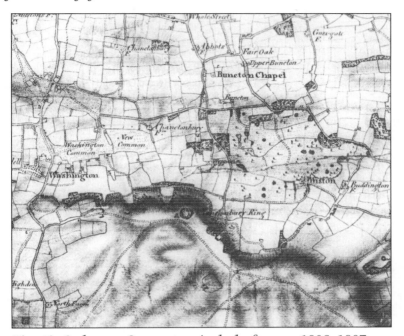

Fig. 40. Ordnance Survey two-inch draft map, 1806–1807.

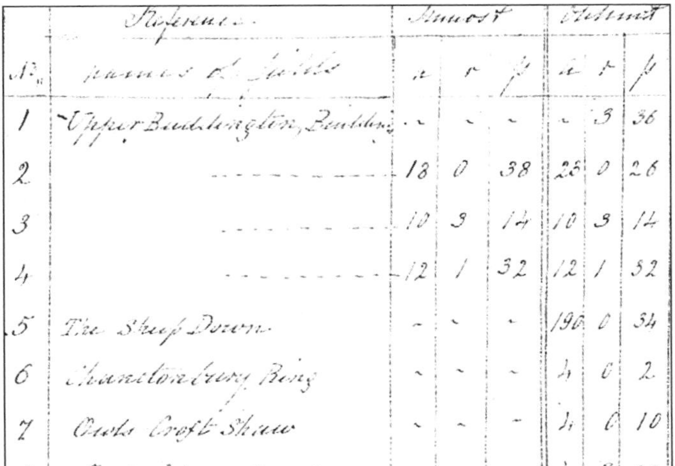

Fig. 41. Legend to map of The South Part of Wiston, c .1825, by William Figg.

The earliest known documentary reference to the hill is in 1351, when it was called the 'hill of Changebury'; this indicates the existence of the hillfort, even though the reference is to the hill. A murder that had taken place there 21 years earlier, in 1330, is discussed in Chapter 4. [13]

The first element of the name Chancton, referring to the farm, or manorial holding, seems to have been Cengel, Changel or Change. In the Domesday Book, 1086, Chancton is written as Cengeltune; in 1230 it was Changethone, then Changetone between 1254-76. In 1300 it was called Sengelton and in 1307 Changeton. The first letter(s) of these variants would have been pronounced 'ch', as in 'chat'. [14]

Back in the mists of time, the base-word was probably *ceangel* or *ceancel* which could be a suffixed form of the word *ceanc* meaning 'lump', found in hill-names elsewhere. So Chancton ('ton' formed from the Old English *tūn* meaning homestead or settlement) is the 'homestead (or farm) at or near Ceangel'. The word Chanctonbury perhaps means the hill or hillfort at or on Ceangel, influenced by the farm name. The hill of Changebury, noted above in 1351, may then translate as the fort or hill (O/E *burh,* fort, fortified place, or *beorg*, hill, mound) of Cengeltune (Chancton). [15] The spelling of the fort/hill part, *burh/beorg*, appears variously as borough, berry, bury and burgh and on a survey of 1587 as Chanckberie hill. [16]

The name spelt as 'Chanklebury', appears in the title of a drawing made from the Petworth area by Edward William Cooke in 1876. The words 'Chanclebury Ring' are sometimes quoted as being an old version of the name, but the first appearance of that spelling seems to be as the title of a poem by Wilfrid Scawen Blunt c. 1880 (see Chapter 5). [17] However, the pronunciation would sit well with the varying names in the previous paragraphs.

In January 1848, in a year when revolutions were breaking out all over Europe, a Roman tile kiln was discovered on the Wiston Estate. Some agricultural workers, employed in draining a field lying a short distance to the north-east of Wiston Rectory, had discovered the remains of a structure built of Roman tiles. Nothing else was found, and William Figg, who wrote a short article about the discovery, was uncertain whether the remains, which he interpreted as a hypocaust for warming the floor of a room, were connected with a Roman bath-house or a villa. [18] Subsequently the remains were identified as the floor and cross walls of the old kiln's firing chamber. [19] The Roman road known as the 'Greensand Way' crosses Sussex from Hardham near Pulborough in the west, to Barcombe, north of Lewes, in the east, probably passing through the grounds of Wiston Rectory, so Roman remains were not unexpected.

In 1867 the Revd James Beck, of Parham Rectory, referring to '...the famous "Chanctonbury Ring" – perhaps the most conspicuous object in our lovely Wealden and South-Down scenery...' writes of the discovery of a hoard of silver coins found on 21 December 1866 at 'Chancton Farm' (now called Upper Chancton Farm), about a mile and a half (2.4 km) to the north of Chanctonbury Ring. The farm labourers apparently '...took away several hundreds, and sold them by handfuls (under the impression that they were tin) for pots of beer'. Of the estimated three thousand coins, which had originally been placed in a leather bag, deposited in an earthen jar and buried, the tenant farmer recovered about 1,600 from his workers, and Beck himself purchased another 200. The coins were handed over to the Treasury and declared 'Treasure-Trove'. [20]

The find was written up in *Sussex Archaeological Collections* in 1868, when it was thought that Chanctonbury Ring was the site of a Saxon encampment. A barn, cattle-shed and yard possibly marked the site of a former farmhouse at Upper Chancton. When the ground was ploughed just before Christmas 1866, the contents of the hoard were scattered in all directions. 'A general scramble took place amongst the labourers on the spot, and twelve pieces of the "old tin" were for a day or two the common price for a quart of beer at the Washington inn' (the *Frankland Arms*). Apparently half a pint of the coins was offered for a quart of 'double X' – no doubt the very good beer from Steyning. The 'intelligent' postmaster of Washington, Mr Cripps, was called in, who found that the coins were silver pennies from the reigns of Edward the Confessor and Harold II. Altogether 1,720 coins were recovered (the numbers do not quite tally with Beck's count, above) and claimed by the Solicitor of the Treasury.

Some of the coins came from the Steyning mint, others from the Lewes and Chichester mints, and they were distinguished by their excellent workmanship. [21]

A 'tradition' apparently connected with the discovery site '...handed down in the neighbourhood from father to son...' was said to be that of an old man with a long white beard, occasionally to be seen around dusk, poring over the ground at Upper Chancton, as if in search of some hidden treasure. Another legend describes an old, white-clad, headless man haunting the spot. [22] Whether the beer from Michell's Brewery in Steyning had anything to do with these stories is unknown. But wait:

> Ye who delight in old Traditions
> And love to talk of apparitions
> Whose chairs around are closely join'd
> Where no man dares to look behind
> Thinking there some Hobgoblin near
> Ready to whisper in his ear.
> Oh listen while I lay before ye
> My well authenticated story... [23]

The Ring-planter, Charles Goring, wrote this in 1802, some 60 years before the discovery of the Upper Chancton hoard. He enjoyed writing poetry, and this very long tale is of twin brothers, Tom and John. They made their fortunes and bought a country cottage, but after some time Tom died, and John was left alone. One night, at the cottage, having drunk too much home-brewed ale and eaten large quantities of gooseberry fool, he had terrible nightmares (unsurprisingly perhaps), and dreamt of phantoms dancing round his bed. One of them was his dead brother, who spoke:

> I come to tell you where to find
> A treasure which I left behind
> I had no time to let you know it
> But follow me and now I'll show it.

With thoughts of gold awaiting him, John followed his brother's ghost to an open field, lately harvested, when 'the spectre pointed to the spot where he had placed the Golden Pot'. The poem becomes coarsely humorous at this point, as John had not brought a spade and sought a way to remind himself where the fortune was buried when he returned in the morning. After his large supper of gooseberries, Mother Nature gave him the answer, and he realised that either his sight or his nose would help him in the morning...but alas, when he returned, the field had been ploughed and the site of the buried riches lost.

Whether this poem was inspired by a treasure-seeking legend current in the Ring-planter's lifetime remains to be discovered.

Colonel Lane Fox (later General Pitt-Rivers) anthropologist and archaeologist, visited Chanctonbury in 1868 when researching hill-forts and barrows on the Sussex Downs. [24] He opened some barrows on the Hill, did not find anything and assumed they were part of the defensive system of the hillfort. These barrows are now considered to date from *c*. 2350 BC, the Early Bronze Age. [25]

In 1909 Charles Goring (1869-1924), grandson of the Ring-planter and owner of the Wiston Estate, had some trenches dug within the hillfort with a view to planting more trees, this time in the central portion of the Ring. The work brought to light considerable quantities of loose flints, many of which were carted away to be used for the walls of a pumping station on the estate. John Butcher, who spent his whole working life on the Wiston Estate, dying in his eighties in 1967, remembered that 'a man' found a lot of coins when carting flints from a spot in the beeches at that time. Butcher said that the man kept the coins and sold them, boasting that '...he got as much as £14 for one coin', a large amount of money in those days. [26]

A long length of wall was discovered, as well as pieces of Roman roof and paving tiles. At that point Mr Goring asked his land agent, George Sharman Mitchell of Broadbridge Place, Horsham, to undertake an archaeological exploration of the open portion of the hillfort. [27] He felt that it should be explored more systematically, to see what kind of building had occupied it. No archaeological excavation had hitherto been made within the Ring. Roman finds had been turning up in the area over the years, and Roman brick or tile can be seen in the walls of Buncton Chapel to the north of Chanctonbury. A Roman road crosses Wiston parish, as mentioned above, and Mitchell therefore expected Roman archaeology at Chanctonbury. [28]

The Ring is an irregular oval enclosure, which Mitchell estimated at about 3½ acres – William Figg, undoubtedly the more accurate surveyor of the two, had estimated that it contained 4 acres and 2 perches.

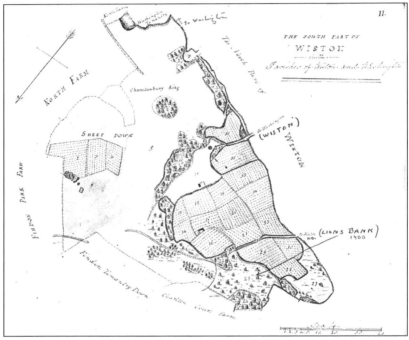

Fig. 42. The South Part of Wiston, c. 1825, by William Figg, annotated by Mr John Goring (1907-1990).

The Ring is clearly shown in Fig. 42 (the tail of the arrow indicates north), with trees not entirely filling the hillfort. Figg has inserted the number 6 within the Ring, which relates to the name 'Chanctonbury Ring' on the map legend in Fig. 41.

Mitchell only noted one entrance into the enclosure, to the south-west of the main works, and seems to have missed the main opening on the north-east. He did comment on the two 'isolated earthen banks [cross-dykes] across the necks of the ridges [of the downland] to the west and to the south-east'. He also noticed that all the buildings uncovered within the hillfort were just a few inches below the surface, consisting of foundation portions of the walls only. A copy of his plan (see Fig. 43) shows the outlines of two 'Roman buildings' – the temples. Interestingly, as mentioned in Chapter 2, he also shows the position of six beech trees, two large ones in the centre of the Ring, either side of the outer wall on the south of what Rudling calls Temple 1 (see Fig. 49), and four more beeches (not described as large) above the site of Temple 2, to the south-west. The dumbbell-shaped depression in front of Temple 1 lay within the hard natural chalk, an apparent pathway about four feet wide and 12 inches deep. Mitchell likened it to a hard track worn by a watchman or sentry pacing up or down, though could not really hazard any other use for it. The U-shaped object reminded him of a military field oven of his time. [29] The little curving track from it led to a circular rubbish pit that yielded a few Roman bronze coins and some pottery, as well as animal bones. The Temple 2 site was not explored fully in 1909, and Mitchell's sketch of it was found to be inaccurate when parts of it were excavated nearly a century later.

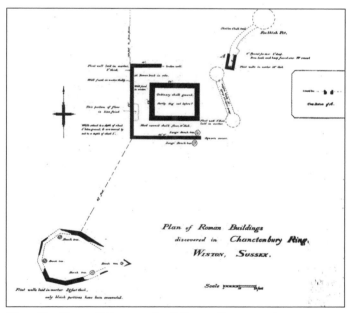

Fig. 43. Plan of Roman Buildings discovered at Chanctonbury Ring, 1909, by G. S. Mitchell. Note the two large beech trees indicated at the temple 1 site, and four at temple 2.

However, accurate or not, Mitchell opened the way to exploring some of the secrets of Chanctonbury Ring before tree-planting covered them up. He presumed that the earthworks were 'of Celtic origin'. During the excavation, 'Mr Goring, of Wiston Park, picked up [a] bronze fibula...It is a Roman brooch belonging to the second half of the first century [AD].' So reported the archaeologists Dr Eliot Curwen and his son in a short article published in 1922. They mention the probable Roman terrace-way that descends the escarpment just to the west of the Ring in the direction of Locks Farm, as well as the one that descends to Owlscroft Barn, presuming that these served the buildings in the Ring. [30]

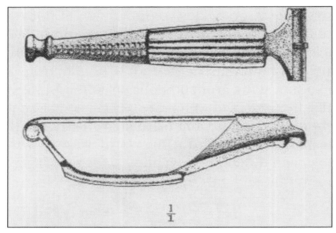

Fig. 44. Roman brooch (a bronze fibula), found during the excavation of Chanctonbury Ring, 1909.

The finds were loaned to Barbican House Museum of the Sussex Archaeological Society at Lewes by Mr Charles Goring. This seems to have led Mr H. S. Toms, curator of Brighton Museum to say 'We have practically nothing from Chanctonbury in this Museum, only one or two Roman tesserae, many of which are turned up in the soil within the camp.' [31] Few Chanctonbury Ring finds remain at Barbican House Museum now. There is one piece of Kimmeridge Shale "Presented by Chas. Goring 1909 with boars tusks etc.', though no tusks are present. There is part of a small bronze pin, and a piece of a bronze fibula, found in 1946. There are a few Roman pottery sherds, with two pieces of tile and two pieces of red wall plaster donated in 1947; some of these are labelled 'Pottery & Tile from the

Roman 'summer-house' within the prehistoric camp of Chanctonbury Ring, Sussex Downs...' [32]

After Mitchell's excavations, Chanctonbury was left in peace for some decades, though archaeologists Drs Eliot and Eliot C. Curwen explored the area in the 1920s and initiated some aerial and other photographs. In 1942, during World War II, Chanctonbury's downland was used by the 142nd Royal Armoured Vehicle Corps (outfitted with 40-ton Churchill tanks) for manoeuvres. The area was also heavily used throughout the war for training purposes by the Canadian Army (encamped in Wiston Park) and other units, particularly in preparation for D-Day. [33]

An Early Bronze Age (*c.* 2100-1700 BC) barrow on the west slope of Chanctonbury Hill was excavated in 1958-59 as it was in imminent danger of destruction by the plough. The skeleton of a young woman was found, lying crouched on her left side, perhaps in her early thirties when she died. A bronze dagger had been placed with the body. There were also remains of a cremation. It was evident that the site had been used during World War II, a military slit trench having been dug there, revealing a 1945 farthing, a round of service ammunition and part of a mortar bomb. [34]

Fig. 45. Cattle at Dew Pond, near Chanctonbury Ring, 1930s.

However, no archaeological exploration took place in the Ring itself between Mitchell's work and archaeologist Owen Bedwin's excavations in 1977. The latter were undertaken because plans had been put forward by the landowner to replant three areas within the clump of trees. Bedwin published his findings in 1980, writing that 'Chanctonbury Ring is situated in the middle of a long, narrow plateau, treeless apart from the Ring itself, and is used for grazing sheep or cattle.' [35] He would have seen the same view, though the clump would not have been so thick, had he been excavating with Mitchell 50 years earlier.

He also commented on the 'enormous hillfort of Cissbury', dominating the view nearly two miles (3km) to the south of Chanctonbury Ring. [36]

Fig. 46. Cisbury [sic] Hill Roman Encampment near Steyning. Sketched August 1820, by W. H. Brooke.

Bedwin repeats the story of the planting of beech seedlings in the second half of the eighteenth century, though mistakenly writes that this was done by the owner, rather than by the owner's son. He states, quoting Mitchell, that the clump has since been carefully maintained. Initially, the centre was left open, the trees growing around and just inside the perimeter of the hillfort. In 1909 it was decided to plant trees in the middle. Bedwin writes that the natural lifespan of the trees in the clump necessitates re-planting 'at regular, though infrequent, intervals'. [37]

He notes that other hillforts in Sussex, those of Highdown, Harrow Hill and Cissbury, can be seen quite clearly from Chanctonbury, though mentions that Cissbury hillfort is much larger, and later in date. Three square Romano-British temples are also known in the county, at Lancing Ring, Bow Hill and Pulborough. A circular structure was found at Muntham Court, Findon, generally accepted as a ritual building of some sort, and a boar plaque was found there, associated with pottery dated to the first to early-fourth centuries AD. [38]

Discoveries at Chanctonbury Ring by Bedwin suggested an earlier Late Bronze Age date for the construction of the hillfort, rather than the previously supposed Early Iron Age, putting it back to *c.* 750 BC. This was later confirmed by Rudling, who also explored the two

Fig. 47. Chanctonbury Ring as viewed from Cissbury Ring, undated but probably c .1930.

temples and discovered large quantities of pigs' teeth and skull fragments in the vicinity of Temple 2. These pig remains indicate that this temple may have been associated with a possible cult of the boar, or a deity associated with boars/pigs. [39] The site may have been abandoned post-AD 370, in the late-Roman period, though absence of finds does not necessarily preclude this. [40]

Archaeological excavation has, of course, progressed in leaps and bounds since Mitchell explored Chanctonbury Ring in 1909 and the great storm of 1987 gave archaeologists the opportunity to investigate the site anew. David Rudling excavated between 1988 and 1991, finding more evidence for the Late Bronze Age dating for the construction and main use of the hillfort enclosure. [41]

Activity on the hill during the Neolithic period (c. 4300–2100 BC) was evidenced by finds of flintwork, and the Early Bronze Age (c. 2100–1700 BC) was represented by four round barrows, pottery and flintwork. There was no evidence for use of the hillfort during the Middle Bronze Age (c. 1700–1300 BC), but by the end of the Late Bronze Age (c. 1300–750 BC) the hillfort, with a single entrance on the north-east side of the rampart, had been constructed. Rudling states that the evidence is typical of sites used for seasonal or intermittent grazing, and of a small number of people, but with no permanent settlement. It was perhaps a corral for domesticated

Fig. 48. Richard Goring, Wiston Estate Manager, with archaeologist David Rudling at the Ring, May 2011.

animals, and may have acted as a centre for the observation and accessing of resources and environments to the north of the Downs. [42]

However, Rudling does not mention a water supply, which would have been critical for animal husbandry. In 1950 protests were made about the erection of an iron water tank on Chanctonbury Hill, but the owner, Mr John Goring, claimed that '....with 600 head of cattle and many more to come, as well as valuable crops, he must have water on tap', indicating that there was no sufficient water supply available in the vicinity then. [43] In 1937 archaeologist Dr E. Cecil Curwen was wondering about supplies for all the Sussex hill-forts. [43] The possible water sources for Chanctonbury have been discussed in Chapter 1.

There was limited Roman activity within the hillfort during the second half of the first century AD, and possibly one, or both, of the masonry temples were constructed during the second century AD. Dating evidence of coins and pottery show that the later building, Temple 2, in the south-west part of the hillfort, had been destroyed by AD *c.* 350. [45]

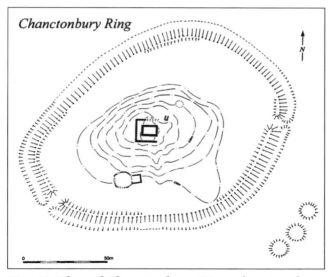

Fig. 49. Plan of Chanctonbury Ring, showing the Romano-Celtic type Temple 1 (in the centre), the Romano-British polygonal Temple 2 (to the south-west) and three Bronze Age roundbarrows (to the south-east), by D. Rudling.

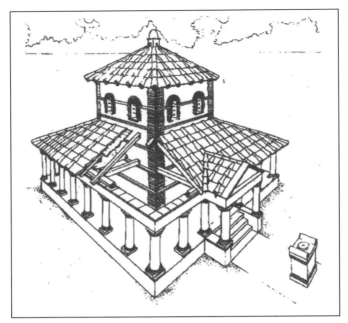

Fig. 50. Temple 1 was possibly similar to this typical
Romano-Celtic temple, drawn by Guy de la Bédoyère.

Fig. 51. Temple 2 may have been something like this
reconstruction of a Romano-British octagonal temple
at Chelmsford, by P. Drury.

In the centre of the Ring, Temple 1, a shrine of a well-known Romano-Celtic type, consisted of a double rectangle with the cult room in the central part, and surrounded by a *porticus* (a covered colonnade, or a long pillared roofed area, backed against the central shrine), providing shelter for worshippers and offerings, and for religious rites. The central part, the *cella*, may have been a tower-like structure rising above the outer wall. This was apparently a suitable form for windy hilltops. It appears to have had painted wall plaster and a tessellated pavement, though the latter had disappeared. There was nothing to identify the cult practised at this temple. [46]

Something should be said here to differentiate between the names 'Romano-Celtic' and 'Romano-British' when referring to these temples. The former term indicates temple types known across the Celtic world, i.e. not only in Britain, but which spread across the Roman Empire, whereas the Romano-British temples were indigenous to this country. Temple 2 is Romano-British, a temple of the Roman period in Britain, and is a polygonal building of nine or eleven sides. [47] This is the building that Mitchell did not have time to explore and which he surveyed inaccurately. An iron spearhead was discovered within it by Rudling, which perhaps represented a votive offering. The tip was missing, and it may have been ritually damaged ('killed') before its placement. This temple seems to have been associated with a possible cult of the boar, as 4,874 fragments of pig bone were found, representing a minimum of 84 individual pig heads – almost all are teeth or pieces of skull, indicating that this assemblage probably results from ritual rather than domestic activities. They have been identified as a mixture of male and female domestic pig, not the wild boar. [48]

At least twelve small boar figurines have been discovered in Sussex, including one at North Farm, Washington, to the south-west, illustrated in Fig. 52. [49] Another (now lost) was found some 20 years ago on Locks Farm, below and to the north-west of Chanctonbury Ring. [50] A copper-alloy boar plaque was discovered at Muntham Court at Findon, a Romano-British temple site (see above). Certainly in this part of south-eastern England there was a significant link between boars, pigs and some temples. The iron spearhead found at Temple 2 may have been associated with either hunting or fighting,

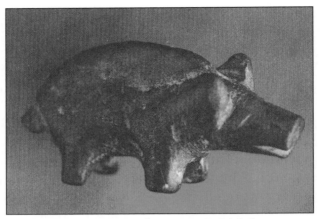

Fig. 52. Late Iron Age/Romano-British bronze
boar, found at North Farm, Washington, Sussex
in 1992. Length 1.2" (3.1 cm), height 0.6" (1.5 cm).

or both. The animal was certainly symbolic of fertility (both agricultural and sexual), and of war. More detail of the temples and a possible boar cult can be read in Rudling's articles. [51] Elsewhere within the Ring, as at the north-eastern entrance, the excavations by Bedwin revealed deposits of sheep and cattle bones (again mainly skulls and mandibles), thus indicating that pig bones were not the only offerings made in Roman times at this sacred site. Elsewhere there was also a large deposit of oyster shells. [51]

Temple 1 was possibly the older and more important of the two. It is on the highest point of the hill and faces the main entrance to the hillfort. Perhaps some time after the official Roman acceptance of Christianity in the fourth century AD there may have been episodes of destruction and robbing of Temple 2. There were Roman villas not far away, at their peak in the middle of the fourth century AD. Rudling feels that perhaps the main patrons of Chanctonbury were converted to Christianity and no longer sponsored pagan cults, or else there was a decline or abandonment of the villa/s associated with this religious complex. [53]

An inhumation burial (that is a burial in a hollowed out trench, the body covered with earth) was found within the hillfort after the 1987 great storm, buried in isolation and away from the temple sites in the Ring. This may have been a murder victim or someone who had been officially executed. The single radio-carbon date could only give a Saxo-Medieval period date. [54]

Mark Tibble's topographical survey of the landscape and hillfort of Chanctonbury Ring was carried out in the summer of 2003 and the winter of 2004, recording previously unsurveyed features that may prove to be Bronze Age round barrows. He has taken a 'new look' at Chanctonbury, interpreting the prehistoric landscape from the Neolithic to the Middle Iron Age and his article is a fascinating piece of detailed research. The technicalities of the survey can be read in volume 146 of *Sussex Archaeological Collections*. Tibble notes that the enclosure is visible for many miles around, constructed on the northern edge of the South Downs; though he does not say that the white chalk of the ramparts, regularly maintained and kept clear of grassy growth, would have added to the intervisibility of many Sussex hillforts. The underlying theme of his interpretation is 'the use of the past by societies in the past'. [55]

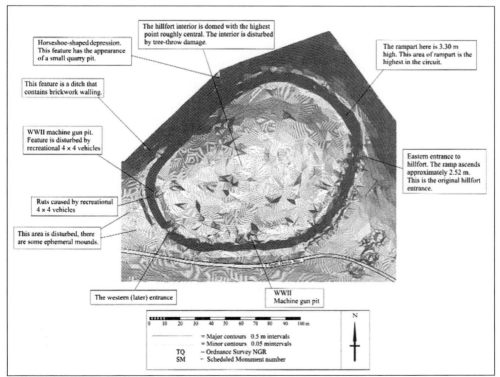

Fig. 53. Topographical survey of Chanctonbury Ring: the hillfort, 2008, by M. Tibble.

After his survey, Tibble says:

> There is no reason why the interpretation of past human communities should be any less complicated than our less than complete understanding of contemporary society...The topographical survey of Chanctonbury has produced pleasing results... [showing] that there was a significant monumental landscape on top of Chanctonbury Hill prior to the Late Bronze Age...' [56]

Since the survey in the winter of 2004 Tibble notes:

> ...recreational use of the landscape is still causing damage to many of the monuments...The metalled track of the South Downs Way is being avoided...by cyclists and 4 x 4 vehicle enthusiasts. Areas of turf adjacent to the track are being eroded and rutted. [57]

He feels that signposting the monuments, or placing notices at the entrance gates would be useful, as then perhaps visitors to the landscape would at least be aware of the nature of the 'lumps and bumps'. [58]

Fig. 54. Horse riders at Chanctonbury Ring, 1930s .

A police raid on the home of a 'nighthawk' living in Kent discovered some objects that had been stolen from Chanctonbury Ring two or three years ago, when a trench was illegally dug inside the Ring. The items have recently been returned to the landowner and comprise Roman pottery sherds and a piece of red-painted wall plaster. There was one medieval sherd from a green-glazed jar or bowl. [59]

It would be as well here to mention that digging on or desecrating a Scheduled Ancient Monument is a criminal offence. Britain's archaeological heritage is being plundered by criminals, usually by metal detecting, and items such as coins and other metallic objects are sold, often on auction websites. Valuable knowledge and finds are thus lost for ever. Sir Barry Cunliffe, Emeritus Professor of European Archaeology at Oxford University (who excavated at Sussex sites such as Muntham Court at Findon and Fishbourne Roman Palace near Chichester), calls for better guidance for police, and a national database to portray the extent of the problem. The offences involved are theft, trespass and contravention of 'The Treasure Act'. There is useful information in the Code of Practice for Responsible Metal Detecting in England and Wales. [60]

However, it should be made very clear that there are thousands of metal detectorists in this country, either working alone or as members of clubs, who enjoy their hobby and act responsibly. Most clubs have a written constitution, with clear rules about reporting finds to the landowner and the relevant authorities. Many metal detectorists help on archaeological excavations, and at other times voluntarily report any finds to the Portable Antiquities Scheme. Many rare and precious items have been discovered by metal detectorists who act in this way; but for them, much of our archaeological heritage would remain unknown. [61]

CHAPTER 4

The Medieval and Later History of Chanctonbury Ring

'...sup[er] montem de Changebury occisus fuit...'
... on the hill of Changebury he was killed... [1]

As mentioned at the beginning of Chapter 3, the earliest documented date for the name 'Changebury Hill' comes from an official enquiry relating to the crown's feudal revenues, which took place in 1351. [2] In order to prove the year of birth, and therefore the 'coming of age' – 21 years – of the heirs to leading families, evidence was sought from inhabitants who had good reason to remember such an event because of something memorable that had happened to them personally at the time of the birth. A court was held at Steyning on 9 April 1351 for evidence to be given in proving the age of John, the son and heir of Edmund, the late earl of Kent (the latter had been executed for treason), so that he could inherit his father's lands and other effects. It was stated that John was 21 years of age on 7 April, and that he had been born at Arundel in 1330. This needed to be corroborated by witness statements. [3]

One of the witnesses was local man Geoffrey Fauconer, who said he remembered the year well, as his son William had been made a monk at Sele (the Benedictine Priory at Beeding, three and a half miles (5.6 km) to the east of Wiston), on 27 May 1330:

> [On the]...eve of the Nativity of St John The Baptist
> [23 June] William went out of the house of La Sele
> against the will of the prior and convent, and in
> going to his friends or elsewhere, was killed on the
> hill of Changebury, as appears by an inquest taken
> about William's death before Gervase de Leem, then
> one of the coroners of Sussex. [4]

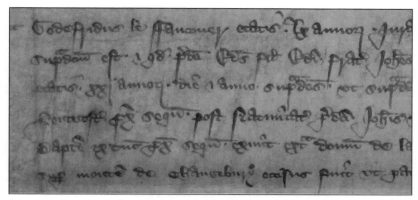

Fig. 55. Geoffrey the Fauconer's evidence at a Proof of Age, 1351 [TNA C135/113/20]. The last line reads 'sup[er] monte[m] de Changebury occisus fuit', i.e. 'on the hill of Changebury he was killed'.

The coroners' inquests from this date do not survive, and it is not possible to say why or how William Fauconer was killed, and exactly where on Chanctonbury Hill this happened. There is no mention of an indictment in the gaol delivery rolls of the period, so it is possible that nobody was brought to trial for the death. The burial mentioned in the previous chapter is unlikely to have been that of William Fauconer, as his body would have been taken to consecrated ground, probably at Sele Priory in Beeding, after an inquest. [5]

Interestingly, there is documentary evidence that a Philip Falconer was possibly living at Wiston in the middle of the thirteenth century, near Chanctonbury Hill, and he certainly had land there. [6] If Geoffrey Fauconer was a descendant, living in the same area, his son William, having become a monk less than a month before, may have been making his way home (without the permission of the Prior) to see his family and friends on St John's Eve (Midsummer Eve) in 1330, when he was murdered. There could have been some festivities organised for 23 June on Chanctonbury Hill that William Fauconer would have known about from past years. The Christian Feast of St John the Baptist was on 24 June, but the lighting of fires on the evening before would have been known to many communities before 1330, and later. The earliest known documentary references to merry-making in England on St John's Eve are from the thirteenth century and the lighting of festive fires was an important part of the ritual. [7] It could be wondered whether William decided to leave Sele Priory against orders so that he could take part in festivities on Chanctonbury Hill. Late in the fourteenth century a monk in Shropshire wrote about the worship of St John on the evening before his Day, when three kinds of fires were lit, involving bones and/or wood, and 'The stench of the burning bones, he added, was thought to drive away dragons.' [8] One of the Washington boundary markers in the AD 963 charter is called 'Wormstall', which probably means 'Dragon's Lair' (see Fig. 35), and could refer to Chanctonbury Ring. [9]

There are no known illustrations of Chanctonbury in the medieval period, but a drawing of 1636 by John Dunstall snr seems to have been copied by Wenceslaus Hollar about ten years later. [10]

Fig. 56. 'Wiston Place and Chankberry Hill', 1636, by John Dunstall snr,.© Leeds Museums and Galleries. All Rights Reserved 2011.

Dunstall snr was working as a military surveyor in Ireland in 1612, and was apparently in Chichester in 1644. He has been identified as the artist of several other Sussex etchings. [11]

Wenceslaus Hollar (1607–1677) was a Bohemian from Prague, whose patron was Thomas Howard, the 2nd earl of Arundel. They met in Cologne in 1636 and the artist joined his retinue, arriving in London the same year. He lodged in Arundel House, London, but two years after his patron went into exile in 1642, Hollar went to Antwerp, not returning to London until 1652. [12] He seems to have acquired a handful of Dunstall's Sussex drawings and may have taken them with him into exile and based at least five etchings on them. It is possible that Hollar never even visited the county or saw Chanctonbury Hill. [13]

Fig. 57. 'Wiston Place and Chankberry Hill', c .1646, by Wenceslaus Hollar, © British Library Board, Maps*14485.(20).

The etching in Fig. 57 shows Chanctonbury Hill standing out against the skyline with its hillfort and fire beacon. [14] Wiston Place, known as Wiston House today, may have been rather 'stretched' by the artist, but various architectural details can be seen, with the church to the left of the house together with the 'long barn' (stables with a granary above) that still remain to the south of the church. In the nearer foreground is Lower Buddington farmhouse with its attendant buildings, all of which were demolished in the 1950s. [15] The line of mature trees below the Downs is on the route of Mouse Lane, leading from the north-west end of Steyning High Street directly to Wiston House.

Chanctonbury Hill is centrally placed, surmounted by the Late Bronze Age hillfort. What can also be seen, situated inside the earthwork, is the stake to hold a beacon, together with possibly a couple of trees to the south, still inside the ramparts, though perhaps it is more likely to be a hut for the fire-watchers. Two temples have been partly excavated within the much earlier earthwork in the twentieth century, but it is possible that there were still above-ground remains at the time of Hollar's depiction of the hill. It could be supposed that the Chanctonbury beacon was constructed on the highest point within the ring, where the first temple had been built. Dr Frank Kitchen, whose research on fire beacons is detailed below, feels that Hollar did not really know what he was copying, judging from the treatment of the beacon in the etching. [16]

Fire signals in England are not documented until the fourteenth century but were noted on the Isle of Wight in 1324, when the sheriffs of nearly every county in England, including Sussex, were ordered to erect them. In 1372 the sheriffs of Sussex, Kent and

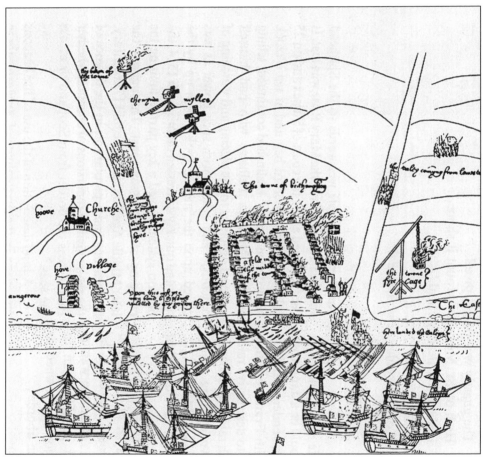

Fig. 58. The French attack on Brighton, 1514. Note the two types of fire beacon, one on the road to Steyning (top left), the other to the east of the town (lower right), on the road to Lewes.

Surrey were ordered to array their forces (prepare for battle) and make the beacons ready without delay. Chanctonbury was recorded as a beacon site in 1587. In 1588, the year of the Spanish Armada, it was planned that 16,000 men would converge on any point on the Sussex coast following the firing of the beacons. In 1640 the south coast beacons were again made ready as the troubled years of the English Civil War approached. [17]

These beacons were simply large bonfires until the reign of Edward III in the fourteenth century, but were gradually replaced by more permanent structures. A tall oak post was erected, rigidly supported, with a ladder or rungs on the post itself to give access to a barrel of pitch or tar-soaked flax mounted at the top. Such a beacon is shown on the 1514 raid on Brighton by the French, [18] and this is probably what Hollar tried to show in his Chanctonbury drawing.

The average distance between beacon sites was about 7 ½ miles (12 km), and some sites were as little as a mile and a half apart (2.5 km). The system evolved over many generations and worked well. Kitchen plots 61 beacon sites in Sussex, though not all were contemporaneous. The Napoleonic beacon at Hollingbury Castle or Camp (hillfort) above Brighton was built on a burial mound inside the earthwork, just as Chanctonbury's beacon was probably built on the highest ground within the earthwork there, near the Romano-Celtic Temple 1 remains. The hill was also a beacon station in 1805, during the Napoleonic Wars. [19]

Chanctonbury Ring was also one of the many sites chosen by Mudge, Williams and Dalby when they carried out their Trigono-metrical Survey of England between 1791 and 1794. They were working in Sussex in 1793, as mentioned in Chapter 3, and beacon sites were ideal trig points for the Ordnance Survey's triangulation. [20] There is a modern trig point on Chanctonbury Hill about 440 yards (400m) west of the Ring, presumably replacing earlier markers.

John Evans describes the beacon on Chanctonbury that he saw *c*. 1813-1814, but obviously felt it could have been better constructed:

> On its *apex*, or top, is a large clump of trees, in the
> centre of which stands a *Beacon*! My curiosity was
> excited – but judge how I felt when I beheld
> something in the form of a sugar-loaf, or rather
> resembling an ill-built rick of hay, leaning different
> ways, and marked only by its deformity. Its extremity
> was thatched to keep off the rain, and the interior is
> stored with combustible materials. Formerly a few
> soldiers lived in a hut close to it, whose province it
> was, with glasses, to keep a watch over the approach
> of the enemy, and in case of actual danger *to fire the
> beacon*; thus giving the earliest alarm and affording
> time to ward off the horrors of an invasion. [21]

This description, published in the year before the Battle of Waterloo, brings home to the reader the anxious years of the Napoleonic Wars and the very real danger of invasion. It also shows that the beacon was not supported in a basket on the top of, or suspended from, a post, but assembled in the form of what we would call a bonfire. Luckily it was not needed. It also indicates that there could not have been many trees in the centre of the Ring at this time.

A bonfire is recorded as being lit on Chanctonbury Hill near the Ring in 1935 for the Silver Jubilee of George V (see above), [22] and in 1953 there was another for the coronation of Queen Elizabeth II. The latter was 23ft high (7.10m), 34ft in diameter (10.36m), and built with 2,250 faggots by John Davey and Les Virgo of the Wiston Estate. Teddy Streeter, another estate worker, slept next to it the night before to make sure it was not lit too early. The 1977 Jubilee Bonfire is mentioned in the Postscript (see below), and the last bonfire to be lit on Chanctonbury Hill was in July 1988 as part of the 'Fire Over England' project. Twenty five feet high (7.62m), it was built by Johnny Goring and a team from the Wiston Estate and North Farm, Washington, to celebrate the 400th anniversary of the Spanish Armada. [23] It mainly comprised trees blown down in the great storm of 1987. Dr Frank Kitchen commented that he spent the evening at the Devil's Dyke from where he could see seven beacons. [24]

Even before the end of the Napoleonic Wars in the nineteenth century, and the need for beacon fires to warn the country of imminent invasion, tourism to Chanctonbury Ring was growing, and with it an outpouring of literary delights which are explored in the next chapter.

CHAPTER 5

A Selection of Literary Sources

'And sitting crowned in the middle place I see Chanctonbury,
which, I think, a dying man remembers so fixed against the south,
if he is a man from Ashurst, or from Thakeham, or from the
pine-woods by the rock, whenever by some evil-fortune a Sussex
man dies far away from home.' [1] H. Belloc

Since the planting of the trees in 1760, Chanctonbury Ring has become one of the most popular landmarks in Sussex and the literary sources are quite overwhelming. Poets, novelists, travellers, ramblers, essayists and musicians have all been influenced by this Sussex landmark. Almost anyone who has written about the county in the nineteenth and twentieth centuries has mentioned Chanctonbury, so this chapter is necessarily selective.

One of the reasons for visiting Chanctonbury is to admire the views on all sides. The northern aspect reveals Kipling's 'wooded, dim,

Fig. 59. View to Wolstonbury Hill, Newtimber Hill, the Devil's Dyke and Truleigh Hill, from Chanctonbury Hill, 2011.

blue goodness of the Weald', to the east the run of the South Downs, where Truleigh Hill, the Devil's Dyke, Newtimber Hill and Wolstonbury Hill can all be seen. The westerly views are extensive on a clear day, even to Portsdown Hill in Hampshire. Southerly views reveal the huge earthwork of Cissbury Ring and the English Channel. Chanctonbury Ring had become a favourite picnic spot by the early-nineteenth century, and a goal for excursions from Worthing. [2]

An account of the rides and excursions from Worthing published in 1814 extols the delights of a visit to 'Chankbury Hill and Ring'. John Evans knew Chanctonbury well, and writes that the '...approach to the ring is rather steep for a carriage, but is perfectly safe', describing the route from Worthing via Sompting, approaching the Ring from the east.

> The trees, although much stinted in their growth, are nevertheless considered an extraordinary phenomenon, when the shallowness of the soil, and the elevation of the hill are considered...[the clump] lays very open to the cutting westerly winds from the Atlantic Ocean, which prevail here during the winter season. The drive to this spot, after leaving the Steyning road, abounds with views of great extent and beauty, but from hence it surpasses all description. It is universally allowed to command the most extensive sea and land view in Great Britain. [3]

Evans goes on to describe the beacon (mentioned in Chapters 2 and 4) in the middle of the clump of trees, where soldiers had formerly been living in a hut close by. He then explains that the view from the Ring is about 125 miles in length and 25 to 30 miles in breadth, commencing at Maidstone in Kent, and terminating beyond Portsdown Hill near Portsmouth in Hampshire. Leith Hill and Box Hill in Surrey are easy to see on a clear day. He also mentions that a cottager and his family resided '...within the ring, near to the beacon' until 'very lately'. Possibly they lived in the hut that had formerly been used by the military, taking care of the beacon and also acting as 'tour guides' to the many visitors, thus earning a few pennies in tips, or they may have supplied services to the soldiers during their guard duties. Napoleon abdicated in April 1814 and was living in exile on Elba by 4th May, which is presumably why the Chanctonbury beacon had been abandoned. After his escape in February 1815 and until his capture a month after the Battle of Waterloo that year, interest in the beacon may have been rekindled.

Evans states that during the season innumerable parties come from Worthing, some for the pleasure of the ride and the views, others for a picnic and the whole day. He continues:

> [the day]...which frequently terminates with a dance upon the velvet lawn...sufficient shade under the foliage is to be found within the ring, and where the horses may be safety tied and refreshed as well as their masters. The delightfully genial and refreshing breeze here in the most sultry day will renovate the valetudinarian and enliven the healthy. The great variety of landscapes and sea views will always attract and interest the observing mind: it seems impossible for anyone to visit this enchanting spot and not return perfectly satisfied with their excursion. [4]

He suggests returning via Findon village, which is about six miles from Worthing.

An account of a picnic on Chanctonbury Ring in 1818, comes from the *Gentleman's Magazine*. 'JF' writes from the Isle of Wight, saying that he had made a personal visit from Worthing last summer, '...to Chanckbury, the Wrekin or Cenis of the South Downs'. Unfortunately the weather was not to be kind to his party. [5]

JF visited 'Chanckbury' in July 1818, wishing '...to form a valedictory commemoration of its picturesque character, noted down for the gratification and refreshment of future reminiscence'. He mentions the 'ring of trees planted by the landholder, Mr Goring of Whiston [sic], within the last thirty or forty years; and if they [the trees] were arrived at maturity, would form no indifferent imitation of an antient Druidical grove'. This is a rather careless statement, as the trees were planted 58 years previously, though does indicate that the trees were not fully grown. In flowing language JF writes of the panoramic prospect of the sea and the '...Wold (or as it is provincially termed, Wild), [the Weald] or low ground of Sussex...The town of Worthing makes a conspicuous part of the beach view.' He notes the old borough of Steyning, and Bramber Castle, and the deer reposing under noble and widespread oaks in 'Whiston' Park, but laments the lack of a river or stream to add to the beauty of the panorama.

His party prepared their picnic, spreading a cloth on the grass and were '...feeding in the Oriental posture...' when they heard the distant rumble of thunder. The clouds approached and the rain fell, so they gathered up their picnic and rushed for shelter '...under the foliage of the Ring, where we sat...' listening to the storm. So presumably the tree cover was mature enough to save them from a drenching, and perhaps they were able to finish eating, though whether 'in the Oriental posture' is not revealed. This was presumably cross-legged, or at least sitting on the ground.

At 8pm they saw more dense clouds gathering in the west and, deciding another storm was on the way, '...we proposed to depart, and mounted horses and vehicles on the other side of the hill'. These had perhaps come as far as they were able from Sompting or Findon. There then follows a vivid description of the descending storm, the tremendous thunder and lightning, the total blackness and atrocious darkness with '...vast and luminous displays of the electric fluid, which frequently dashed the horses, and dimmed their vision by its supreme brilliancy, as it appeared to roll along and ignite the earth under our feet.' However, with cheerfulness and fortitude, they continued on their way (or rather the drivers did) back to Worthing.

In September 1822 Horatio Smith (1779-1849), writer and humorist, purported to have spent a week in Worthing, writing about his stay with some verve. His essay is written in the character of a Cockney grocer of Tooley Street, and to say he found Worthing boring would be an understatement. After braving one of the bathing machines, losing a stocking and banging his elbow, he decided to visit Chanctonbury Ring:

> Donkey cart again. Chanctonbury Ring. Driver said
> finest prospect in the world. Asked him how much
> of the world he had seen? Answered, "Lancing,
> Shoreham, and Broadwater Green". Donkey jibbed at
> foot of hill. Got out and dragged him up by left ear.
> Fine exercise for a valetudinarian. Let his ear go, and
> found that it did not move with the other. Afraid I
> had dislocated the organ. Paid driver three and
> sixpence, and said nothing about it. Dined upon cold
> beef. Appetite on the decline. [6]

What a pity that he did not describe the actual Ring and its 'prospect'. [7]

In 1866, five years after the death of Prince Albert, the Revd John Goring had been thinking of building a Swiss Cottage in the Ring for his children. Queen Victoria and Prince Albert had bought Osborne House on the Isle of Wight in 1845, and rebuilt the house in 1848. The Swiss Cottage that was built in the grounds in 1853–1854 as an educational tool for the royal children (domestic skills for the girls, carpentry and gardening for the boys) had resulted in many similar ideas across the country. The royal Swiss Cottage was built in Alpine style of pine, 50ft x 25ft (15.24m x 7.62m), of two storeys, with a balcony, garden and thatched summer-house. Elizabeth Trower, half-sister to the Revd John (and 25 years older than him), did not think much of this idea. She wrote to him at Wiston in June 1866 from Germany, where she was travelling with her husband Walter Trower, the bishop of Gibraltar, saying:

> We did receive your letter about the Swiss Cottage on
> Chanctonbury but could hardly think you in earnest
> in such a scheme which amuses us not a little. You
> will find it would never answer the purpose of sea
> air for your children, who want bracing, & should be
> as near the waves as possible for much benefit to
> them. Chanctonbury would scarcely be less relaxing

than Worthing is & how often is there thick fog over it even when it does not reach Wiston. What does Isabel [the Revd John's wife] say to it? [8]

No more is heard about a Swiss Cottage on Chanctonbury Ring, perhaps unsurprisingly, as by the mid-nineteenth century at least two Worthing entrepreneurs were organizing trips to the Ring by horsedrawn charabanc or omnibus, and it might not have been a very suitable place for the Goring youngsters to be 'braced'. [9]

The Ring obviously looked lovely in spring time, as in May 1868 Sir William Eden was writing amusingly to the Revd John Goring, congratulating him on returning from Brighton:

...in recovered Health and spirits to enjoy the ever changing beauties of this lovely springtime among your own greens & lawns, which after the dust & wind of dreary Brighton must be doubly pleasant. How beautiful must the *Grand Mamelon* [the Big Nipple] look now, clothed in the bright yellow of the Beech woods'. [10]

Fig. 60. Chanctonbury Ring, South Downs, 1883, by A. Elliot.

Fig. 61. Chanctonbury Ring, South Downs, 1883, by A. Elliot.

The 1883 illustration by Elliot, above, looking northwards to the Weald, shows a seated figure under the trees. Whether this is a shepherd sheltering from the rain (he seems to be wearing some sort of hat with a flap at the back, and a cloak) is uncertain. Perhaps it is the artist himself or a companion. There is an odd-looking piece of timber in the middle ground, beyond the seated figure, but it is difficult to make out just what it might be. It could possibly be a signpost pointing to distant landmarks in Sussex and surrounding counties.

Louis Jennings (1836-1893), journalist and politician, had been the special correspondent of the London *Times* in India and the United States. He was eventually editor of *The New York Times* and on returning to England in 1876 became a prolific rambler. In his rambling book about Surrey and Sussex he only gives a short mention of Chanctonbury Ring, writing that 'it is said to be an earthwork of Celtic origin, planted round with trees'. [11] In his book about Derbyshire and the South Downs there is an illustration of Wiston House and Chanctonbury (see Fig. 63), though the artist has possibly placed another clump of trees to the east of the Ring, or else rather exaggerated the downland there. [12]

Fig. 62. Pamela Platt sitting under an old beech tree at Chanctonbury Ring, 1 August 2010.

Fig. 63. Wiston Park, c. 1880, by A. H. Hallam Murray.

Jennings writes:

> The ring of trees on the summit of Chanctonbury
> Hill forms almost a part of the park, with all the
> woods and fields which lie between. The great
> ornament of Chanctonbury, its crown of trees, was
> given to it by the father of the Rev. John Goring, the
> present owner of Wiston, and ever since the trees
> were first planted they have been carefully watched
> and tended, and replaced when decay began to work
> mischief. It was an excellent idea to plant these trees
> on Chanctonbury, and it is an interesting fact that
> Mr Charles Goring lived to see them reach their full
> beauty. He set them out in 1760, and sixty-eight
> years afterwards – on 15 December, 1828 – he
> addressed the following lines to the hill on which he
> had placed what it is to be hoped will be a perpetual
> landmark. [13]

He then quotes the Ring-planter's poem, with its ungrammatical
'Beech and sides'. Jennings climbed to Chanctonbury Ring and
describes it as follows:

> To begin with, he [the rambler] will notice that the
> ring of trees, which can be seen from so many miles
> away, is planted on a circular mound, within an
> outer trench – it is, in fact, an ancient earthwork,
> British or Roman, no one knows which, and stands
> 814 feet above the sea level. There is an outer
> rampart of trees, which serves to some extent to
> shield the inner circle, consisting of larches, [14] from
> the fury of the winds. Many of these outer trees are
> curled into all kinds of distorted shapes, and bear
> heavy marks of the warfare against the elements
> which they almost constantly have to wage. But the
> inner circle is formed of straight and well-grown
> trees, and young saplings have been planted on the
> west to afford them further protection. Chancton-
> bury Ring is much too picturesque a feature in the
> landscape to be allowed to perish. [15]

He recounts that Box Hill can be seen, also the tower on Leith Hill in Surrey, across the Weald. 'On clear days it is said that Windsor Castle and Tunbridge Wells can be made out.' He also notes Wolstonbury Hill and the inn on Devil's Dyke. [16]

> Let him who has a sorrowful or disturbed mind go to
> some such spot as this above the ancient park of
> Wiston, and sit down quietly, and dwell upon the
> scene around him. Kind mother Nature will softly
> come with her healing hand; the clouds will gradually
> be lifted; the wounds which the troubles or anxieties
> of life have made will cease to smart, even though
> they are too deep to be healed. Amid such scenes,
> the freshness of the mind comes back again...Of all
> the South Downs walks, I am disposed to give the
> palm to the one between Steyning and Amberley.
> Let the reader put down this book and go forth upon
> it for himself – he will be dissatisfied with the writer
> who has so inadequately attempted to describe it,
> but he will thank him for suggesting the means of
> adding to his life at least one delightful day. [17]

Richard Doddridge Blackmore (1825–1900), novelist and fruit farmer, is well-known for his novel *Lorna Doone*, a best seller in 1870. He is less well-known for *Alice Lorraine: A Tale of the South Downs*, which was published in three volumes in 1875. It was badly received, but on reading it today (no easy task) it can be seen that 'Westward of that old town Steyning, and near Washington and Wiston, the lover of an English landscape may find much to dwell upon.'

The tale, set partly in the early-seventeenth and partly in the mid-nineteenth century, need not bother the reader here, but Blackmore must have visited the area, indeed must have stayed for a while to do research at Bramber and around the Adur valley. He obviously appreciated the well-known landmark of Chanctonbury Ring '...the scene of many a merry picnic...' and describes it in his novel as a '...salient point and foreland of a long ridge of naked hills, crowned with darker eminence by a circle of storm-huddled trees'. He describes market day at Steyning and has his character Alice talk about 'Chancton Ring', describing the ancient trees as:

> ...a vegetable throng of weather beaten and fanastic
> trunks...of no great size...Yet, from their countless
> and furious struggles with the winds in their might
> in the wild midnight, and from their contempt of aid
> or pity in their loneliness, they enforce the respect
> and the interest of any who sit beneath them.

Alice (*alias* Blackmore) describes them as 'Weymouth pines and Scottish firs'; he may have muddled the former with Norway spruce. There is no mention of beech trees. [18]

The Revd Francis Kilvert (1840–1879), diarist, made a short visit to Sussex in 1874. He stayed in Worthing for a few days in order to attend a friend's wedding at Findon, where he met a young lady by the name of Kathleen Mavourneen, one of the bridesmaids. The 34 year old Kilvert immediately fell in love with her – though he was to marry another five years later – and his diary entry of 11 August 1874 reminds him that he visited the Ring with Kathleen and others after the wedding:

> In the afternoon almost all the wedding party went
> up to that fine clump and height of the Downs called
> Chanctonbury Ring. Part of the way we drove and
> we walked up the steepest part. Kathleen was still
> my sweet companion. Under the lee of the clump I
> spread my coat on the turf and we sat there together
> on the hillside apart from the rest and looked over
> the wide and glorious landscape, bright plain and
> green pasture, blue hill and golden corn and stubble
> fields, till she could see over rich and variegated
> plain the white line of the Grand Stand on Epsom
> Downs some 30 miles away. And there we sat and
> talked and looked into each other's eyes and there I
> fell in love and lost my heart...Chanctonbury, sweet
> Chanctonbury, thou wilt always be a green and
> beautiful spot in my memory. [19]

Fig. 64. Looking north to Surrey from Chanctonbury Hill, 2011.

Wilfrid Scawen Blunt (1840-1922), hedonist, poet and breeder of Arab horses, wrote a short poem *c.* 1880 entitled 'Chanclebury Ring', though the spelling of the name may have been an invention of his own which has been copied in later years by other writers. However, in 1876 an artist named Edward William Cooke drew a distant view of Chanctonbury Ring from the Petworth area, using the spelling 'Chanklebury' in his title. [20] He and Blunt (the latter born at Petworth House) may have known each other, or perhaps Blunt knew Cooke's drawing and adopted the alternative spelling of 'Chanclebury' for the poem he wrote four years later.

Blunt was buried in the woods of his Sussex home, Newbuildings Place, Southwater, with some lines of his poem engraved on his tomb there, serving as his epitaph. The complete poem does not in any way describe the Ring, but refers to the view '...from this upper down...Dear checker-work of woods, the Sussex weald.' [21] Blunt must have visited Chanctonbury Ring on various occasions, and certainly did so in the summer of 1906, writing in his diary in June:

> On Saturday we made an expedition to Chanclebury Ring, I in my wheeled chair with a donkey, the others in the American trap, and we took luncheon with us. While we were there, a horseman rode up who turned out to be Goring, from Wiston, who is the owner of the Down, and we renewed acquaintance. He told us, among other things, that his father's and his grandfather's lives together covered 180 years, their tenure between them of the Wiston Estate 150 years. [22]

Blunt and his party had met Mr Charles Goring, grandson of the Ring-planter of the same name. The Revd John Goring, his father and the Ring-planter's son, had died the previous year.

In 1902 poet and author Hilaire Belloc (1870–1953) walked across Sussex, writing about his journey in *The Four Men: A Farrago*, which was published in 1912. Though alone, he had three invented companions with him, the Poet, the Sailor and Grizzlebeard, all facets of his own personality. After stopping at the *Swan* inn at Pease Pottage, just south of Crawley, the four men (though in fact only Belloc) walked about a mile to '...that place where the wood upon the left ends sharply upon that height and suddenly beneath one's feet the whole County lies revealed. There, a day's march away to the south, stood the rank of the Downs'. [23] Grizzlebeard says (as mentioned earlier):

> And sitting crowned in the middle place I see Chanctonbury, which, I think, a dying man remembers so fixed against the south, if he is a man from Ashurst, or from Thakeham, or from the pine-woods by the rock, whenever by some evil-fortune a Sussex man dies far away from home. [24]

They stay the night in a house not far from the *Fountain* inn at Ashurst, whose beer was provided by the Steyning United Breweries. After a while the other three settle down for the night by the fire, but Belloc himself is wakeful, going outside to watch the world:

The moon stood over Chanctonbury, so removed and cold in her silver that you might almost have thought her careless of the follies of men; little clouds, her attendants, shone beneath her worshipping, and they presided together over a general silence. Her light caught the edges of the Downs. There was no mist. She was still frosty-clear when I saw her set behind those hills. The stars were more brilliant after her setting, and deep quiet held the valley of Adur, my little river, slipping at low tide towards the sea. [25]

Belloc had grown up at Slindon in Sussex, and in 1906 bought his house King's Land on the upper reaches of the river Adur at Shipley, near Horsham, where he lived until the end of his life. He particularly enjoyed the beer from Steyning United Breweries and would have appreciated the view of Chanctonbury Ring from the *Frankland Arms* at Washington. Belloc's 'West Sussex Drinking Song' was inspired by the beer at various Surrey and Sussex pubs, 'But the swipes they take in at Washington Inn is the very best beer I know.' [26]

Fig. 65. Chanctonbury Ring across the river Arun, south-west of Henfield, September 2011.

Edward Verrall Lucas (1868-1938) came to Brighton with his parents not long after he was born, and thus felt able to call himself a Sussex man. He became an essayist, biographer and travel writer, and his *Highways and Byways in Sussex*, (1904), with illustrations by Frederick L. Griggs, is a delightful ramble through the Sussex countryside. His words begin the Introduction to this book:

> ...when one thinks of the South Downs as a whole it is Chanctonbury that leaps first to the inward eye. Chanctonbury, when all is said, is the monarch of the range...It is Chanctonbury's crown of beeches that lifts it above the other hills...its dark grove can be seen for many miles. [27]

Fig. 66. Chanctonbury Ring, c .1904, by F. L. Griggs.

Lucas quotes the Ring-planter's poem, perpetuating the mistake of '...new-clothed Beech and sides...', instead of 'beechy sides' (see Chapter 1). He also writes that 'Most of the trees on the side of Chanctonbury and its neighbours were self-sown, children of the clumps which Mr Goring planted', though the Ring-planter was an inveterate arboriculturalist and is reputed to have planted many of the beech hangers on the Downs at Wiston and Washington. [28]

Matthew Coombe was born on the Wiston Estate in 1864, second son to Benjamin Coombe the gardener. He wrote three known poems, which were printed in an undated booklet called *Memoirs of Wiston by a Sussex Yokel*. The Revd John Goring, who died in 1905, is mentioned in 'A Sussex Harvest Home'. [29] Coombe left Wiston and moved to town, as in 'Downland Calling' he writes:

> Goodbye to Chanctonbury and Downland fair!
> Fain would I pay the heavy debt I owe
> For days of joy and peace in thy sweet air.
> I humbly bow my thanks – Goodbye! – and
> Townward sadly go

In 'My Downland Home' he recalls in later life the beauty of his Sussex surroundings:

> Fair Chanctonbury! With sylvan glory crown'd,
> And lovely Wiston nestling at thy feet,
> Where shall I find thy peer, the whole world round,
> Or charming grace that weaves a spell so sweet?

Rudyard Kipling (1865–1936), writer and poet, lived at Rottingdean, near Brighton, from 1897 until 1902 when he purchased Bateman's at Burwash in the Sussex Weald. Many of his poems and stories are set in Sussex, but he only seems to have mentioned Chanctonbury Ring by name once, in a short poem 'The Run of the Downs', in his children's book *Rewards and Fairies*, published in 1910:

> *The Weald is good, the Downs are best-*
> *I'll give you the run of 'em, East to West,*
> Beachy Head and Winddoor Hill,
> They were once and they are still,
> Firle, Mount Caburn and Mount Harry
> Go back as far as sums'll carry,
> Ditchling Beacon and Chanctonbury Ring,
> They have looked on many a thing,
> And what those two have missed between 'em,
> I reckon Truleigh Hill has seen 'em... [30]

The poem continues, naming the downland hills as far as the Hampshire border. His story 'They', in *Traffics and Discoveries* (1904), published separately in 1905, reveals that he had come close to Chanctonbury Ring on a car journey (he always had a chauffeur) he made from Burwash to Washington. His eldest daughter Josephine, had died in 1899 at the age of six, and his loss is intertwined with this story of children living in a house under the South Downs. Kipling's car journey begins at Bateman's, and continues below:

> [I]...let the county flow under my wheels. The orchid-studded flats of the East gave way to the thyme, ilex and grey grass of the Downs: these again to the rich cornland and fig-trees of the lower coast, where you carry the beat of the tide on your left hand for fifteen level miles; and when, at last, I turned inland through a huddle of rounded hills and woods I had run myself clean out of my known marks. [31]

He passes through the Findon valley to Washington, and other hidden villages, seeing 80 foot lime trees overhanging grey Norman churches, brooks and stone bridges, tithe-barns and an old smithy, as well as a Roman road:

Fig. 67. Chanctonbury Ring Road near Steyning, c .1920.

As the wooded hills closed about me I stood up in the car to take the bearings of that great Down whose ringed head is a landmark for fifty miles across the low countries...A quick turn plunged me first into a green cutting brim-full of liquid sunshine; next into a gloomy tunnel where last year's dead leaves whispered and scuffled about my tyres. The strong hazel stuff meeting overhead had not been cut for a couple of generations at least, nor had any axe helped the moss-cankered oak and beech to spring above them. [32]

One could imagine making one's way up the deep Chanctonbury Ring Road to the foot of the downs, or perhaps in sunken Mouse Lane, approaching Wiston House from Steyning. The ancient house that Kipling, or his character, discovers at the end of the lane, with its mullioned windows and weather-worn stone, and particularly his glimpse of an octagonal dove-house could make one presume that he was using the environs of Wiston House for his model.

Fig. 68. Octagonal dovecote at Wiston House.

Michael Smith writes that the description of the entrance hall to the house '...is clearly based on that at Bateman's and the ornate topiary of the garden.' Kipling brings topiary peacocks into his story, which could be based on one at a house he may have known near Tunbridge Wells. [33] However, *They* is just a story, though a magical one based on memories of his deceased daughter, very moving indeed, but using his car journey to the Wiston area and the landmark of the 'ringed head', Chanctonbury Ring.

Arthur Beckett, whose family owned a newspaper group in their name, published in Eastbourne, Worthing and other Sussex coastal towns, wrote an extremely popular book, *The Spirit of the Downs*. It was published in 1909 and went through eight reprints. Beckett was the founding president of the Society of Sussex Downsmen, and was also editor of the *Sussex County Magazine* for many years. Jacqueline Simpson thinks that Beckett probably began the story of walking seven times around the Ring without stopping, when the Devil will come out and hand the walker a bowl of soup; this is discussed below. [34]

In June 1916, during World War I, a poem named 'Chance Memory' or 'From Steyning to the Ring' was published in the *Daily News*. The name of the poet was given as Philip Johnson, and the poem is one that deeply moves many readers:

> I can't forget the lane that goes from Steyning to the Ring
> In summer time, and on the downs how larks and linnets sing
> High in the sun. The wind comes off the sea, and oh, the air!
> I never knew till now that life in old days was so fair.
> But now I know it in this filthy rat-infested ditch,
> Where every shell must kill or spare, and God alone knows which.
> And I am made a beast of prey, and this trench is my lair –
> My God, I never knew till now that those days were so fair,
> And we assault in half-an-hour, and it's a silly thing:
> I can't forget the lane that goes from Steyning to the Ring. [35]

'Philip Johnson' was in reality John Stanley Purvis (1890–1968), who became canon Purvis of York, famous for his versions of the York mystery plays. He was the first director of the Borthwick

Institute of Historical Research. His poem is dated 2 December 1915, when he was about to leave for service in World War I, having been a teacher at Cranleigh School in Surrey. It was not written in the trenches of France, as might be supposed. Lynda Denyer of Steyning Museum has done a considerable amount of research on the origins of the poem and its author, and the full story can be read in the Steyning Museum Newsletters of October and December 2009. It should just be mentioned here that in the author's original manuscript, now at Steyning Museum, the last line of the poem reads 'I can't forget the narrow lane to Chanctonbury Ring'. [36] There is no evidence to show when or how Purvis visited the area, but he could have caught a train to Steyning from Cranleigh. [37]

In the autumn of 1917 children's writer Eleanor Farjeon (1881-1965) rented a cottage near Amberley in Sussex, living alone there for two years. Her most memorable work, *Martin Pippin in the Apple-Orchard*, was published in 1921 and established her as a writer. Part of her story is set around the village of Washington and she writes of the South Downs '...on the highest of which you will see a ring of beech-trees.' She uses the names of many of the farmhouses on the Wiston Estate in her chapter called 'The King's Barn'. [38]

Some scenes are set on and around Chanctonbury Ring, using one of the dewponds there for a moonlight bathing drama. The hero of one of Martin Pippin's stories, young King William, is told to keep a vigil 'between the two great beeches in the middle of the Ring' (an interesting reference, perhaps, to the two large beeches in Mitchell's drawing, see Fig. 28 in Chapter 3). At sunset:

> ...he set forth to mount the great hill with the sacred
> crown of trees upon its crest. When at last he stood
> upon the boundary of the Ring, his heart sprang for
> joy in his breast, and his breath nearly failed him
> with amazement at the beauty of the world which
> lay outspread for leagues below him. [39]

After various adventures in and around a dewpond where he meets a beautiful naked woman, he kneels down between 'the two mid-most beeches' within the Ring. Readers will be pleased to know that there is a happy ending.

Many people will remember the 1967 BBC2 adaptation of *The Forsyte Saga* by novelist and playwright John Galsworthy (1867–1933), but how many remember, in this tale of love and treachery, that it was on Chanctonbury Hill that the ill-fated romance between Fleur and Jon began? *The Forsyte Saga: To Let* was published in 1921, and one of the characters, Val Dartie, had leased '...an old manor house...on the north side of the Sussex Downs'. The hills were a delight to him and his family; his daughter Holly loved '...to go up there by the ravine-like lane and wander along toward Chanctonbury or Amberley...' In Chapter Eight of *To Let*, 'Idyll on Grass', Galsworthy (who lived for some years at Bury in Sussex) describes the walk that Fleur and Jon (played by Susan Hampshire and Martin Jarvis) took to Chanctonbury Ring. Jon had a passion for birds, but 'in Chanctonbury Ring there were none – its great beech temple was empty of life, and almost chilly at this early hour, they [Fleur and Jon] came out willingly again into the sun on the far side.' When Fleur was singing, 'The larks joined in, sheep-bells, and an early morning church far away over in Steyning.' Galsworthy must have known the area well. [40]

Fig.69. The southern bank and ditch of Chanctonbury Ring, 2011.

Pamela Platt remembers in particular Fleur and John:

> ...running down the track hand in hand...it was an aerial shot with the helicopter/plane moving away so that eventually you got a shot of the whole landscape with them as tiny figures still running away downhill...just to the west of Chanctonbury Ring...and perhaps why I remember it so vividly is that it was such a dramatic photographic technique. [41]

A brief mention is made here of a neglected English poet, Charles Dalmon (1872–1938), born in the parish of Old Shoreham and educated at Washington village school. His topographical Sussex poetry will soon be more widely known. A book of Dalmon's poetry, *A Poor Man's Riches*, published in 1922, has the following dedication: 'With The Love of a Lifetime I Dedicate My Poems To Chanctonbury The Most Beautiful Of All The Downs.' [42]

Fig. 70. Beech roots at Chanctonbury Ring, 2011.

Archaeologist A. Hadrian Allcroft writes about Chanctonbury Ring in *Downland Pathways* in the early 1920s. He incorrectly refers to a Sir John Goring as the Ring-planter, rather than the young Charles Goring, but says that 'to miss it [the Ring] is to miss one of the gems of Sussex, nay, of England' referring to the hillfort as being littered with brick, tiles and pottery. He mentions '...the big dew-pond that was made not 50 years ago...' and 'Hevend Gate' (which was known locally as Heaven's Gate) to the east, and the Roman terrace-way to the west, where there is '...a weird and wizened lime-tree that might have stood sentry here when Vespasian was young...' [43] Sussex archaeologists, Drs Eliot and Eliot C. Curwen (father and son), had also spotted this lime-tree and photographed it about the same time, though it was not part of the Ring.

Fig. 71. Dr Eliot Curwen looking at the old lime tree by the Roman trackway to the north west of Chanctonbury Ring, c. 1929.

Robert (Bob) Thurston Hopkins, the founder of the Society of the Sussex Downsmen, felt in 1927 'It is worth climbing up to the Ring on a May morning solely to hear the call of the cuckoo. From the thickets at the foot of the hills cuckoos call continuously...' He mentions a local proverb: 'Old Mother Goring's got her cap on – we shall soon have wet...' meaning that when mists obscured the Ring the rain would soon follow. He also says:

> I am not a Sussex man myself, but in spite of the fact I can never see Chanctonbury Ring in the 'blue distance' without feeling a thrill in my blood. It has an enchantment – a sort of elemental sweetness – which is not easily explained. The Ring is not merely a topographical fact to me – it is ten thousand Sussex men who sleep in Flanders...it is part of the race-consciousness. The spell of Chanctonbury is the very innermost significance, the truest wealth of England...It is the heritage of the sons and daughters of Sussex, and with its magic has won our hearts to a passionate devotion.' [44]

John Ireland (1879–1962), composer and organist, loved the Sussex downland, having taken rooms in Ashington, to the north of Washington village, in the early 1920s. He made notes on his walks and worked on his compositions, many relating to Sussex, in his Chelsea studio later. In 1930 he published *Piano Sonata*, the third movement of which (*Con Moto Moderato*) was inspired by Chanctonbury Ring. *A Downland Suite* was published in 1932. In 1953 Ireland was able to buy Rock Mill at Washington, even nearer to Chanctonbury than his Ashington rooms, and he lived there until his death in 1962. [45]

A rather charming short poem about Chanctonbury by F. Edwin Hodder was published in the *Sussex County Magazine* in 1932:

> On loftiest peak of South Down land
> The Chancton lamp is fixed,
> A Roman eagle's nest; God's hand
> The camp with trees has mixed.
> The great roots darkly groan and rend,
> Reveal the ramparts round:
> And wild the haunted branches bend,
> Glooming all the ground. [46]

Philip Gosse (1879–1959), general practitioner and writer on natural history, also a founder member of the Steyning Preservation Society (now the Steyning Society), lived at a house in the parish of Wiston called Weppons. This house, not very well disguised as 'Crossbows' in his book *Go to the Country* (1935), is situated below and to the north of Chanctonbury Ring. He writes of opening the window of his bedroom on a moonlit night, with '...the great sombre hill, silent and asleep, its contour silhouetted against the star-bespattered heavens.' He describes a stormy winter's day with fierce gales blustering and roaring up the Channel, when Chanctonbury 'is magnificent' and when the white sea fog, looking like fleece from below:

> ...reaches the crest and encounters the Ring and passes through its leafless trees like bleached wool through a carding comb. The advancing cloud goes silently on to pour down the steep side of the hill until it reaches and envelops the line of tall Scotch firs which form our boundary...Naturally the Ring is haunted. Even on bright summer days there is an uncanny sense of some unseen presence, which seems to follow you about.

He repeats the tale that 'No birds live in this sombre wood but a single pair of yaffles [green woodpeckers], and occasionally the silence is broken by a loud, mocking laugh.' [47]

Journalist and children's writer Arthur Mee (1875–1943) can probably be blamed for the continuance of Mitchell's story of the bottles of water supposedly carried by Ring-planter Charles Goring to sustain his trees. Mee's delightful book on Sussex, part of *The King's England* series, was first published in 1937 and went through numerous reprints. In the first edition, he writes about *The Man Who Planted Chanctonbury Ring*:

> It was he [Charles Goring] who planted the beeches that have made Chanctonbury Ring famous for miles around; he planted them as saplings and would climb the hill day by day to keep them watered. [48]

Ten years on the watering has taken on a life of its own, and Mee is writing:

> There is a charming path to his trees from Washington,
> and as we take it we may think of this boy toiling up
> it 170 years ago with his seedlings, and toiling up it
> day by day, week by week, month by month, year by
> year, with bottles of water for them to drink. [49]

The carrying up of water bottles (and they would not have been made of plastic) for several hundred trees is a pleasing romantic tale, but makes no practical sense whatsoever, as discussed in Chapter 2.

Amongst many other books, Nancy Price (1880–1970), actress and author, wrote *Jack By The Hedge*, published in 1942. She was told by one of her vagabond friends that if she went to Chanctonbury Ring alone and at midnight, she might meet the Devil, and that to see the sunrise there would be "summat warth the unbeddin!" As she had never seen either, she thought the experiences would provide a memory worth having, though she was not so sure about the Devil. She kept her eyes open while walking towards Chanctonbury, but saw no sign of him. She only saw a devil's coach-horse, but not liking beetles, avoided it. She thought he would probably be in disguise, and as she approached the Ring her small dog was fiercely excited and expectant. A frightened bird flew up in front of her with a startled cry; an owl hooted; she lost the track but stumbled her way 'towards the Devil's observation post...' [50]

> At last, puffing and blowing and thinking what a fool
> I was, I reached the Ring. Chanctonbury had never
> seemed so far. Scant of breath and laughing at my
> folly, I threw myself down, wishing I were twenty
> years younger. Even as I wished this, I knew the
> Devil could not be far away and that he was judging
> my weakness. [51]

This might be the place to mention, briefly, a book published in 1987 called *The Demonic Connection*, relating to Cissbury, Chanctonbury and the Sussex village of Clapham. Unfortunately the history of Wiston House and the Sherley family within it is inaccurate, and there are no footnotes to indicate the sources of the author's historical information, but if anyone wishes to read about UFOs, levitation and white-bearded Saxons at Chanctonbury, this is the book to choose. [52] The white-bearded Saxon story did not originally belong to the Ring, but has been 'moved' to Chanctonbury from Upper Chancton Farm, where the Anglo-Saxon coin hoard was discovered in 1866 (see Chapter 3). However, as Simpson relates (below), the legend of the Devil appearing at the Ring cannot be traced before 1909. [53] It seems to be a twentieth century invention.

Wendy Dixon, now living in Ontario, Canada, spent her early childhood in Steyning and much later wrote of the early years of World War II, '...like being stuck in Chanctonbury Ring for over six hours one glorious afternoon, because there were continual dog-fights overhead. We went there for a walk and a picnic, and ended up picking untold pounds of blackberries in the Ring while the troubles went on above us.' [54] A copy of her memoir, 'When Canada Came to Help Britain', can be found in Steyning Museum. [55]

Fig. 72. Chanctonbury Ring, Wiston Pond and Wiston House, snow scene, 1947.

Shortly after World War II ended, F. C. Dunford was writing poems about Chanctonbury and many other Sussex places dear to his heart. His two albums were donated to Worthing Local Studies Library in 2001, and contain poems from 1947 to 1987. They are written in a delightful hand with many sketches of birds, flowers, plants and buildings, also landscapes and people, illustrating the poems. Some of the poems are based on R. D. Blackmore's *Alice Lorraine*, mentioned above, though there are others, and he also includes background notes. He writes that his poetry was inspired by rambles with a friend, Otto Pattrick, who died in 1949 and was the cousin of the late Revd Pattrick, rector of Washington (1897–1936). He mentions that Otto often walked to Worthing Library and back from Washington, about 20 miles. Dunford noted a memorial to a Goring family member in Sullington church, to the west of Washington, and in 1971 wrote:

> Edward Goring's slab, a giver to the poor:
> Whose seed in less than a 100 years from then
> Produced the land-mark's famous Beechy Ring
> Putting matured beauty to poetic pen. [56]

This Edward Goring lived at Cobden, Sullington, a distant relative of the Ring-planter. His 'seed' was not, however, involved in the tree-planting, as he died childless in 1683. [57]

Charles Grigg, a Steyning grocer and market-gardener, published some memories in the 1960s, his words about Chanctonbury Ring reflecting the thoughts of many local people:

> ...certainly one of the distinguishing features of the
> neighbourhood and is thought of with affection by
> all who have lived within sight of this tree-covered
> hilltop. To such a one, returning maybe after a long
> absence, Chanctonbury Ring is the first landmark
> that he looks for. To many an airman born in Sussex,
> returning perhaps from a dangerous mission over
> enemy territory during the last War, it was often this
> well-remembered clump of trees, spotted when
> crossing the coast of his native county, that told him
> he was not far from home. [58]

My father Eric Holden was at Kalyan Transit Camp in India with the Royal Engineers during the latter part of World War II, and, aged 33, wrote to his wife, my mother Hilda, on 9 June 1945. He told her how much he missed her love and companionship (they had married in Hove in 1938), going on to say:

> I should like to be home with you, now, and if I
> were, we would have an excursion into the country,
> perhaps with Janet, and we would go somewhere
> like Steyning or Storrington, and climb up the green
> bostals to the triumphant heights of the South
> Downs...I think now, of our last journey to
> Chanctonbury, when the thick enveloping mist
> swathed the hill tops, but which lifted while we were
> at the Ring, allowing us to descend in fair visibility.
> These thoughts are not nostalgic to me, as I realise
> it is useless to indulge in wishful thinking, but they
> act as an anchor when one feels weary and far from
> home.' [59]

Dr Jacqueline Simpson, the Sussex folklore expert mentioned above and in Chapter 1, published a well-researched and interesting article on the 'Legends of Chanctonbury Ring' in 1969. She mentions, amongst various local stories, the eeriness of the Ring, though reminding readers that there is quite a contrast between the warm open downland on a sunny day, and the dim, chilly, silent clump of trees where the thick coverage (before the 1987 storm) cut out all sound. The spot is also subject to sudden mists and low cloud.

As mentioned above, she thinks that Arthur Beckett began the story of the Devil. His popular book, *The Spirit of the Downs*, was published in 1909 (though the article about the first archaeological excavation at the Ring in that year, with an associated Roman temple, was not published until 1910) and went through eight reprints. He wrote 'If, on a moonless night, you walk seven times round the Ring without stopping, the Devil will come out of the wood and hand you a basin of soup...'. Simpson says that this story '...flourishes orally with many variations...' and gives some examples collected by her in Worthing in 1968 and 1969. As the Devil legend cannot be traced before 1909, Simpson writes 'That the Chanctonbury Devil is a dim memory of a Romano-Celtic god is an attractive hypothesis, but no more.'[60]

The autobiography of Mervyn Stockwood (1913-1995), Anglican priest and bishop of Southwark, is named *Chanctonbury Ring*, though he only refers to it a few times. However, he found the Ring a place of solace and inspiration:

> On New Year's Eve I walked on the Sussex Downs to Chanctonbury Ring. Since my undergraduate days it had been a favourite haunt of mine and I try never to make a decision of importance without turning matters over in my mind as I wander around the Ring.

He made a pilgrimage there one year with David Sheppard, one of his suffragan bishops (later the bishop of Liverpool) and Sheppard's wife.

> In the summer I was often alone with my thoughts on Chanctonbury Ring...On New Year's Day 1981 I walked the Sussex Downs to Chanctonbury Ring...Something happened: I don't know what. The depression of several years was lifted and I found inward happiness and peace...

Fig. 73. Chanctonbury Ring on a damp day, from the west, Summer 2010.

The book has a photograph of the bishop with Malcolm Muggeridge at the Ring in 1982, and the undated back cover photograph shows Stockwood looking at the Ring from the east. His ashes were scattered there in 1995. [61]

So many people have written about the Ring and even more have been part of its enchantment. There can be no better ending for this chapter than the words of Sussex author and historian Peter Brandon, writing in 1998. They ring out for the majority of people who love the county and the South Downs:

> By its presence felt for miles around, Chanctonbury has acquired a mystical and symbolic force without equal in southern England. Its recent replanting will ensure that the magic of its ancientness and sanctity will inspire future generations. [62]

Fig. 74. Chanctonbury Ring, from the east, the new trees growing up within the old, Spring 2011.

Fig. 75. Janet Pennington at Chanctonbury Ring, April 2011.

Postscript

Chanctonbury Ring '...has a history that lasted through prehistory and is still being written today.' [1] M. Tibble

One of the events for the Silver Jubilee of Queen Elizabeth II was the lighting of a bonfire at Windsor Castle on 6 June 1977. On that damp and drizzly summer evening, my husband Martyn and I, with some friends, climbed the bostal to Chanctonbury, where the Wiston Jubilee bonfire awaited. Helped by local residents, the staff of North Farm, Washington had taken six hours to build the enormous bonfire, after which they stood guard until 10pm. The core was filled with redundant beechwood from the Ring and the mound was 23ft (7.01m) tall, 33 ft (10.05m) across and 115 ft (35.05m) in circumference. It was not one of the 103 official bonfires linked with the one the Queen fired at Windsor, but nonetheless very well attended by crowds of local people and other visitors. Fires were apparently burning on Devil's Dyke to the east and at Chantry Hill, Storrington to the west, but it was so misty that it was difficult to see these and the rest of the downland beacon fires. Soon after 10pm Lady Hersey Goring, wife of Mr John Goring whose great-grandfather Charles planted Chanctonbury Ring's beeches and other trees in 1760, lit the great bonfire with a red, white and blue torch. A beacon blazed from Chanctonbury Hill for the first time for many years and the crowd spontaneously burst into patriotic songs; our party was in good voice due to some home-made elderberry wine. Despite the damp weather, it was a wonderfully inspiring evening, as the bonfire blazed and crackled on the magical hill. The evening was rounded off by a stumbling descent by the steep chalk track, slippery with rain, after the celebrations were over. We had forgotten to bring a torch, as had many others, so crashes and cries from those who tripped over tree roots or simply lost their way echoed through the moonless night, as we made our way home. It was a very special evening, long to be remembered.

Fig. 76. Janet Pennington's parents Hilda and Eric Holden excavating at the deserted medieval village of Hangleton, Hove, Sussex, c 1953. [2]

Acknowledgements

I am most grateful to many people for help and advice. In particular Harry Goring, owner of the Wiston Estate, and his son Richard Goring, the Estate Manager, have been most enthusiastic supporters of my research on Chanctonbury Ring, offering practical help, documentary and photographic evidence, as well as reminiscences and encouragement. David Rudling, Senior Lecturer in Archaeology at the University of Sussex, who excavated at Chanctonbury Ring 1988-91, has visited the site with me on two occasions. He has been most generous in answering my numerous questions, thus saving many errors and omissions. Richard Coates, Professor of Linguistics, University of South West England (formerly of the University of Sussex), has patiently answered my queries about the place-names Chancton and Chanctonbury. Christopher Whittick, Senior Archivist, East Sussex Record Office, has kindly explained the 'Proofs of Age' system and has also alerted me to nuances of language in the medieval period. David Arscott of Pomegranate Press has seen me through the editing process with patience and humour.

I also wish to thank the following friends, colleagues and advisers: Caroline Adams, Senior Archivist, West Sussex Record Office; Dr Peter Brandon, for inspiration; George Cockman, Charles Dalmon researcher; Peter Drewett, Professor of Archaeology; Martin Hayes, County Local Studies Librarian, West Sussex County Council Library Service; Dr Frank Kitchen, Sussex fire beacon expert; John Mills, Senior Archaeologist, West Sussex County Council; Alison McCann, Assistant County Archivist, West Sussex Record Office; Robin Milner-Gulland, Emeritus Professor, University of Sussex; Christine Payne, Monumental Inscriptions Officer, Sussex Family History Group; Fiona Robertson, Research Professor of English Literature, Birmingham City University; Steyning Library staff; Mark Tibble, Archaeologist; David Thompson, Researcher, Steyning Museum; Chris Tod, Curator, Steyning Museum.

Several people have given help with illustrations and advice about copyright, for which I am very grateful: Sandra Powlette of the British Library; Seren Langley of the Council for British Archaeology; Nigel Brown of Essex County Council, Historic Environment Branch; David Standing, the Gilbert White Museum; Zoe Lubowiecka of Hove Library; Paul Wilkinson of Kent Archaeological Field School; Nigel Walsh and Theodore Wilkins of Leeds Art Gallery; Imogen Lyons and Alexandra Ault of the National Portrait Gallery; Philip Hunt of the Scottish National Portrait Gallery; Luke Barber, Esme Evans and Chris Milburn of the Sussex Archaeological Society.

Guy de la Bédoyère, historian and archaeologist, and Paul Drury, archaeologist, have both kindly allowed me to reproduce their drawings in order to illustrate the types of Romano-Celtic and Romano-British temples that may have stood within Chanctonbury Ring.

About seven years ago, the Wiston History Girls (of which research group I am a member), Jane Goring Page, Janine Harvey, Joyce Sleight and Jill Turner (or the Five Jays) began the task of transcribing several hundred eighteenth and nineteenth century letters relating to the Goring family of Wiston. They have been an unfailing source of information, humour and support during my research, and Joyce has kindly read the text, offering grammatical and practical advice.

Pamela Platt, my sister, and Scheduled Ancient Monument Monitor for the Chanctonbury Ring area, and Bob Platt, my brother-in-law and local naturalist, have accompanied me to Chanctonbury Ring on various occasions over the last eighteen months, counting tree roots, taking photographs, searching for wells and ponds, being stung by nettles and pricked by brambles. They have both given generously of their time and expertise in the Sussex landscape and environment. Pamela has also read the text with an eagle eye. My husband Martyn, whose knees have not allowed him to walk up to Chanctonbury Ring for some time, has been a steadfast supporter throughout my research.

Fig. 77. Pamela and Bob Platt at Chanctonbury Ring, April 2011.

Bibliography

Abbreviations

SAC Sussex Archaeological Collections
SRS Sussex Record Society

Primary sources

British Library, Maps*14485.(20.), Wiston Place, *c.* 1646, by Wenceslaus Hollar.
Census Returns 1841-1901 for Steyning, Washington & Wiston.
East Sussex Record Office, LIA/3/1, 2, Letter in the Attic project, 128 letters
 written by Eric Holden to Hilda whilst he was en route to, and stationed in,
 India in the Royal Engineers from April 1945 to February 1946; Hilda Holden
 wrote 87 letters in return.
Leeds Museums and Galleries, 13/28a/53, Wiston Place and Chankberry Hill,
 12 February 1636, by John Dunstall snr.
Letters in private hands: the Revd John Goring to Elizabeth Trower, post 1861;
 Elizabeth Trower to the Revd John Goring, 14-15 June 1866; Sir William Eden to
 the Revd John Goring, 4 May 1868.
Letter from Frank Kitchen to Eric Holden, received 21 May 1987.
Letter from John Jolliffe to Joyce Sleight, April 2009.
The National Archives, C135/113/20, Proof of Age; JUST 3/123, Gaol Delivery
National Maritime Museum, PAE5529, 'The South Downs and the Sussex
 Downs from Gorehill House, near Petworth, with Chanklebury Ring', 1876, by
 Edward William Cooke.
West Sussex Record Office, Acc. No. 15920, 'Wiston Estate: Woods''; OH 65, taped
 interview with Mrs Win Garrett by Janet Pennington and Joyce Sleight, 1988;
 OH 86, taped interview with Mr John Goring by Janet Pennington, 1990;
 Ordnance Survey 25" Sheet 51 (6), revised in 1897 but first surveyed after 1875;
 Ordnance Survey Map, Sheet 51, 1" to the mile, 1879 (1883); Par. 211, 1/2/1,
 1/3/1-2, 1/3/4, 1/5/1, Wiston Parish Registers; PM 283, Draft Ordnance Survey
 2" map, *c.* 1806-1807; Wiston MS 3658, 1 May 1649, Conveyance (bargain and sale)
 of the Manor of Wiston and other properties, in consideration of £6,870, from
 John [2nd] earl of Thanet, and Margaret, his wife, to John Fagge of East Hoathly esq.;
 Wiston MS 5517, Letters, 28 September – 3 October 1786, some draft, between
 Charles Goring of Wiston to [the Revd] Roger Clough Esq. of Warminghurst Park,
 disputing possession of downland at Chanctonbury Ring; Wiston MS 5602, Wiston
 1801, A Plan of the Old Parsonage House & Glebe, also the New Parsonage House
 & Glebe; Wiston MS 5611-5638, Maps of farmland, part of the Wiston Estate, *c.* 1825,
 in Ashington, Ashurst, Upper Beeding, Steyning, Washington and Wiston, surveyor
 not stated, but almost certainly by William Figg; Wiston MS 5661, 1909, ground
 plan of old building discovered in Chanctonbury Ring, by G. S. Mitchell; Wiston
 MS 5759, Agreement, 1 June 1906, between Charles Goring and George Sharman
 Mitchell of Broadbridge Place, Horsham, whereby the latter is appointed agent of
 the Wiston estates...'

Printed primary sources

Booker, J.M.L.,(ed.), *The Wiston Archives, A Catalogue*, (1975).

Farrant, J., 'Sussex Depicted: Views and Descriptions 1600-1800', *SRS* **85**, (2001).

Freeth, S., (ed.), *The Wiston Archives, Vol 2, A Catalogue*, (1982).

Kingsley, D., 'Printed Maps of Sussex 1575-1900, *SRS* **72**, (1980-1981).

Secondary sources

Allcroft, A. Hadrian, *Downland Pathways*, (1924, 2nd edn).

Anderson P. & McKenna, K., *West Sussex Literary Trail*, (2007).

Banting, D. R., *William of Muntham: A Nabob of Sussex*, (1984).

Beckett, A., *The Spirit of the Downs*, (1909).

Belloc, H., *The Four Men: A Farrago*, (1952 reprint).

Bernieres, L. de *Notwithstanding: Stories from an English Village*, (2009).

Blackmore, R. D., *Alice Lorraine: A Tale of the South Downs* (undated reprint, *c.* 1922).

Blunt, W. S., *My Diaries: Being a Personal Narrative of events 1888-1914*, Pt 2, (5th edn, n.d.).

Brandon, P., *The South Downs*, (1998).

Clifford, J., *Capability Brown: An illustrated life of Lancelot Brown 1716-1783*, (1992 reprint).

Coates, R., *The traditional dialect of Sussex: A historical guide, description, selected texts, bibliography and discography*, (2010).

Coombe, M. 'Downland Calling', *Memoirs of Wiston by a Sussex Yokel*, (n.d. ?post 1920).

Copper, B. *Across Sussex with Belloc: In The Footsteps of 'The Four Men'*, (1994).

Curwen, E. C., *Prehistoric Sussex*, (1929); *The Archaeology of Sussex*, (1954, 2nd rev. edn)

Dictionary of National Biography (2004-2011), articles on (Joseph) Hilaire Pierre René Belloc by Bernard Bergonzi; Richard Doddridge Blackmore by Charlotte Mitchell; Wilfrid Scawen Blunt by Elizabeth Longford; Lancelot Brown by John Phibbs; Sir John Fagge by J. T. Peacey; John Galsworthy by Geoffrey Harvey; King George III by John Cannon; Wenceslaus Hollar by Robert D. Harding; John Nicholson Ireland by Fiona Richards; Louis John Jennings by H. C. G. Matthew; Francis Kilvert by A.L. Le Quesne, rev. Brenda Colloms; (Joseph) Rudyard Kipling by Thomas Pinney; Sir Thomas Lawrence by Michael Levy; Edward Verrall Lucas by E. V. Knox, rev. Katharine Chubbock; Augustus Henry Lane Fox Pitt-Rivers by Mark Bowden; (Lillian) Nancy Bache Price by John Elsom; Horatio [Horace] Smith by Fiona Robertson; (Arthur) Mervyn Stockwood by Michael De-la-Noy.

Dunford, F. C., *Chanctonbury Idylls*, (1947-1987).

Ekwall, E., *The Concise Oxford Dictionary of English Place-Names*, (1960, 4th edn).

Evans, J., *Picture of Worthing, to which is added An Account of the Adjacent Villages, and of the Rides and Excursions in its Vicinity*, 2 vols, (1814).

Harrison F. & North, J. S., *Old Brighton, Old Preston, Old Hove*, (1937).

Farjeon, E., *Martin Pippin in the Apple Orchard* , (1952 edn).

Galsworthy, J., *The Forsyte Saga: To Let*, (1921).

Gelling, M., *Place-Names in the Landscape: The geographical roots of Britain's place-names*, (1993 edn).

Grigg, C. A., *Memories of Steyning*, (1967).

Gosse, P., *Go To The Country*, (1935).

Hewitt, R., *Map of a Nation: A Biography of the Ordnance Survey*, (2010).

Hudson, T. P., (ed.), *A History of the County of Sussex*, 6, Pt 1, (1980).

Hutton, R., *The Stations of the Sun: A History of the Ritual Year in Britain*, (1996).

Jennings, L. J., *Field Paths and Green Lanes in Surrey and Sussex*, (1884, 4th edn); *Rambles Among the Hills: In the Peak of Derbyshire and the South Downs*, (1880).

Kipling, R., *They*, (1905); 'Sussex', *Rudyard Kipling's Verse, Inclusive Edition 1885-1926*, (1929, 4th impression); *Rudyard Kipling's Verse, Definitive Edition*, (1973).

Lace, I., *John Ireland*, (1997).

Lucas, E. V. *Highways and Byways in Sussex*, (1904).

Mawer, A. & Stenton, F. M., *The Place-Names of Sussex*, Pt 1, (1929).

Mee, A. Sussex: *The Garden by the Sea*, (1937, & 1947 reprint).

Newton, T., with C. Walker & A. Brown, *The Demonic Connection: An Investigation into Satanism in England and the International Black Magic Conspiracy*, (1987).

Parish, Revd. W. D. *A Dictionary of Sussex Dialect*, (1957 edn), originally published in 1875.

Plomer, W., (ed.), *Kilvert's Diary 1870-1879: Selections from the Diary of the Rev. Francis Kilvert*, (1964 edn).

Price, N., *Jack By The Hedge*, in M. D. Francis (ed.), *The Sussex Bedside Anthology*, (1950).

Rackham, O., *Trees and Woodland in the British Landscape* (1983 reprint).

Rowell, C., *Petworth House*, (The National Trust, 1997).

Salzman, L. F., *The Chartulary of Sele*, (1923).

Smail, H., *The Worthing Road and Its Coaches* (1943).

Smith, M., *Kipling's Sussex*, (2008).

Stockwood, M., *Chanctonbury Ring*, (1982).

Stratton, J. M. & Houghton Brown, J. (ed. R. Whitlock), *Agricultural Records A.D.220-1977*, (1978).

Stroud, D., *Capability Brown*, (1984 edn)

Thurston Hopkins, R., *Sussex Pilgrimages*, (1927).

Weller, L. & Whiteley, P. (eds), *Sussex and the Grand Tour: A Loan Exhibition of paintings and other works of art from collections in Sussex and neighbouring counties*, (1986).

Wilkinson, G., *Trees in the Wild and Other Trees and Shrubs*, (1983 reprint).

Worledge, J. W., *Systema Agriculturae*, (London, 1687, 4th edn).

Articles in books and journals

Beck, J., 'Remarkable Discovery of Saxon Coins at Washington', *SAC* **19**, *Notes & Queries*, (1867), 189.

Bedwin, O., 'Excavations at Chanctonbury Ring, Wiston, West Sussex 1977', *Britannia* **11**, (1980), 173-222.

Cooper, W. D., 'Proofs of Age of Sussex Families, Temp. Edw. II to Edw. IV', *SAC* **12**, (1860), 23-44.

Curwen, E. & Curwen, E. C., 'Covered Ways on the Sussex Downs', *SAC* **59**, (1918), 35-75 ; 'Some Roman Antiquities – Wiston, Chanctonbury, and Cissbury', *SAC* **63**, *Notes & Queries* (1922), 220-21.

Figg, W., 'On the Remains of a Roman Building discovered at Wiston in 1848', *SAC* **2**, (1849), 313-15.

Godfrey, J., 'Local Government in the 19th and 20th Centuries', in K. Leslie & B. Short, *An Historical Atlas of Sussex*, (1999), 126-27.

Kitchen, F.,'The Ghastly War-Flame: Fire Beacons in Sussex Until The Mid

17th Century', *SAC* **124**, (1986), 179-91.

Lane Fox, A. H., 'An Examination into the Character and Possible Origin of the Hill Forts of Sussex' *Archaeologia* **42**, (1869), 27-52.

Lucas, J. C., 'The Hoard of Anglo-Saxon Coins Found at Chancton Farm, Sussex', *SAC* **20**, (1868), 212-21.

McWhirr, A., 'Roman tile-kilns in Britain', in A. McWhirr, (ed.), *Roman Brick and Tile: Studies in Manufacture, Distribution and Use in the Western Empire, British Archaeological Reports, International Series 68*, (1979), 97-189.

Milner-Gulland, R.,'The Washington Estate: New Evidence on an Ancient Boundary', *SAC* **143**, (2005), 205-14.

Mitchell, G. S., 'Excavations at Chanctonbury Ring, 1909', *SAC* **53**, (1910), 131-36.

Ratcliffe-Densham, H. B. A., 'A Woman of Wessex Culture', *SAC* **106**, (1968), 40-48.

Rudling, D, 'Chanctonbury Ring revisited: The excavations of 1988-91', *SAC* **139**, (2001), 75-121; 'Roman-period Temples, Shrines and Religion in Sussex', in D. Rudling (ed.), *Ritual Landscapes of Roman South-East Britain*, (2008), 95-138.

Smith, H., 'Select Society: or, a Week at Worthing', *The Worthing Parade*, **No. 2**, (1954), 12-29.

Simpson, J., 'Legends of Chanctonbury Ring', *Folklore* **80**, (Summer 1969), 122-31.

Tibble, M., 'A topographical survey of Chanctonbury Ring, West Sussex: An Interpretation of the Prehistoric Landscape from the Neolithic to the Middle Iron Age', *SAC* **146**, (2008), 53-73.

Magazines, Newsletters and Newspapers

The Gentleman's Magazine, 89, (1819).

New Monthly Magazine, 4, (1822).

Steyning Museum Newsletters, (October & December 2009).

Sussex County Magazine: **Vol. 6, no. 9**, (Sept. 1932); **Vol. 9, no. 12**, (Dec. 1935) ; **Vol. 10, no. 1**, (Jan. 1936); **Vol. 15, no. 10**, (Oct.1941); **Vol. 16, no. 2**, (Feb. 1942); **Vol. 24, no. 1** (Jan. 1950).

West Sussex County Times, 22 July 1988.

West Sussex Gazette, 3 June 1971; cutting dated '1978', in private hands; 21 August 1980; 2 January 1988; 2 & 7 September 1989.

Typescript

Dixon, W, 'When Canada Came to Help Britain', (1999), Steyning Museum Archives, World War II.

Thesis

Godfrey, J., 'Ownership, Occupation and Use of Land on the South Downs Between the Rivers Arun and Adur in West Sussex, *c*. 1840–*c*.1940', 2 vols, unpublished DPhil, University of Sussex, (1999).

Websites

www.britarch.ac.uk
www.musicweb-international.com/ireland
www.stonepages.com/news

Notes

Foreword

1 Louis de Bernieres, *Notwithstanding: Stories from an English Village*, (2009), 94.
2 Bostal or Borstal: this is a southern dialect word for any steep track up the northern escarpment of the South Downs, see Revd. W. D. Parish, *A Dictionary of the Sussex Dialect*, (1957 edn), 11, originally published in 1875.
3 Parish, 151, Widdershins – Going contrary to the course of the sun.
4 R. Kipling, 'Sussex', *Rudyard Kipling's Verse*, (1973, Definitive Edn), 214.

Introduction

1 E. V. Lucas, *Highways and Byways in Sussex*, (1904), 145-46.
2 A. Mee, Sussex: *The Garden by the Sea*, (1947 reprint), 391-92.
3 B. Copper, *Across Sussex with Belloc: In The Footsteps of 'The Four Men'*, (1994), 72.
4 The South Downs National Park was opened on 31 March 2010; West Sussex County Council (hereafter WSCC), SMR 4324-MWS5184; Ordnance Survey Map Reference TQ 1395 1210.
5 D. Rudling, 'Chanctonbury Ring revisited: The excavations of 1988–91', *Sussex Archaeological Collections* (hereafter *SAC*) 139, (2001), 75.
6 The replanting was undertaken by the Wiston Estate, aided by a grant from WSCC.
7 See J. Godfrey, 'Local Government in the 19th and 20th Centuries', in K. Leslie & B. Short, *An Historical Atlas of Sussex*, (1999), 126-27, for the intricacies of boundary arrangements between the western and eastern areas of Sussex.

Chapter 1

1 M. Coombe, 'Downland Calling', *Memoirs of Wiston by a Sussex Yokel*, (n.d. ?post 1920); Matthew Coombe was a son of the gardener at Wiston; see West Sussex Record Office (hereafter WSRO), OH 65, taped interview with Win Garrett (née Carter) of Wadhurst, West Sussex, formerly of Wiston, by Janet Pennington and Joyce Sleight, 1988.
2 WSRO, Par. 211, 1/2/1, 1/3/1-2, 1/3/4, 1/5/1, Wiston Parish Registers. In 1867 a Miss Sarah Ann Wilmer (who would have been about 20 years old) is mentioned as being a teacher at Wiston School, in a letter (in private hands) dated 21 March 1867 from Frances Trower, in Malta, to her aunt Isabella Goring, married to the Revd John Goring of Wiston.
3 Personal comment by Mr R. H. Goring.
4 Letters and painting in private hands; the latter was loaned to Sotheby's in 1986, for an exhibition, 'Sussex and the Grand Tour', to help raise funds for the restoration of Chichester Cathedral. The book accompanying the exhibition, L. Weller & P. Whiteley (eds), *Sussex and the Grand Tour: A Loan Exhibition of paintings and other works of art from collections in Sussex and neighbouring counties*, (1986), 25, displays a black and white copy of the portrait of Charles Goring, with the accompanying text: 'The portrait was originally painted with the sitter holding a brace of partridges. These were later replaced with a volume of *Virgil*'. This statement is incorrect, as Mr R. H. Goring says that his great-great grandfather was originally holding a woodcock by its beak, and the artist's replacement for this was a volume of Homer's works.
5 J. Clifford, *Capability Brown: An illustrated life of Lancelot Brown 1716–1783*, (1992 reprint), 25.

6 The Ring-planter's father had been given the middle name of Matthew, presumably by his mother, née Matthews, daughter of Admiral Sir George Matthews, though the 's' was dropped.

7 WSRO, Wiston Mss 3658; *Dictionary of National Biography*, (2004-2011) (hereafter *DNB*), article on Fagge by J. T. Peacey.

8 The baronetcy descended via the son of his first marriage to Mary Blackborne.

9 The present landholding is *c.* 6,300 acres, information from Mr R. H. Goring; see John Godfrey, 'Ownership, Occupation and Use of Land on the South Downs Between the Rivers Arun and Adur in West Sussex, c.1840-c.1940', 2 vols, unpublished DPhil, University of Sussex, (1999), 184-88, for land in Wiston and Washington parishes owned by the Ring-planter's son, Charles Goring, in 1840.

10 See D. Stroud, *Capability Brown*, (1984 edn); DNB, article on Brown by John Phibbs.

11 C. Rowell, *Petworth House*, (The National Trust, 1997), 52-53; J. Farrant, 'Sussex Depicted: Views and Descriptions 1600-1800', *SRS* **85**, (2001), 53, writes 'The shift in perception had already been advanced by landscape gardening in the style of 'Capability' Brown which prompted planting on the Downs, as on Chanctonbury Ring in 1760...'

12 A letter from John Jolliffe to Joyce Sleight of Steyning, April 2009, relates that the son of William Jolliffe of Ammerdown, T. S. Jolliffe, knew Charles Goring the Ring-planter well, as they had been at school together. Jolliffe's family history records that 'a fourth chimney-piece from Egrement House (in London and owned by the 3rd earl of Egremont 1763-1790s) was obtained by Mr Goring of Wiston', though the date of this event is unknown; there are no letters or accounts relating to the Goring family in the Petworth House Archives, according to archivist Alison McCann.

13 The coronation of George III took place in September 1761, though his accession was in October 1760.

14 J. M .Stratton & J. Houghton Brown, (ed. R. Whitlock), *Agricultural Records A.D.220-1977*, (1978), 79-80.

15 L. N. Candlin, 'Chanctonbury site for magic cauldron?', *West Sussex Gazette*, (21.8.1980); nineteenth century Census Returns and BMD records list several males named John Butcher born in Washington.

16 E. Cecil Curwen, *Prehistoric Sussex*, (1929), Plate XXV (RAF photograph).

17 WSRO, Ordnance Survey 25" Sheet 51 (6), revised in 1897 but first surveyed in 1875, only shows two dewponds.

18 *West Sussex Gazette*, (3 June 1971), 9.

19 *Sussex County Magazine* (hereafter *SCM*), **16, no. 2**, (Feb. 1942), 59.

20 J. W. Worledge, *Systema Agriculturae*, (London, 1687, 4th edn), Chapter X also gives details of making '...Pools of Water on Hills and Downs for Cattle...'; F. Grigg, *Memories of Steyning*, (1967), 24–25, remembers that there were at least eight dewponds within the triangle of downland bounded by Steyning Round Hill, Cissbury and Chanctonbury Ring.

21 These would now be called 'Highland Cattle'.and they grazed the Ring and Wiston Park when Mr John Goring was young, in the earlier part of the twentieth century (personal comment by Mr R. H. Goring).

22 'Chanctonbury Dew Ponds', *SCM*, **15, no. 10**, (Oct.1941), 333–34; areas of Clay-with-Flints occur naturally within the chalk downland.

23 'Chanctonbury Dew Ponds', *SCM*, **16, no. 2**, (Feb. 1942), 59.

24 A. H. Lane Fox, 'An Examination into the Character and Possible Origin of the Hill Forts of Sussex' *Archaeologia* **42**, (1869), 42-44.

25 E. Curwen & E. C. Curwen, 'Covered Ways on the Sussex Downs', *SAC* **59**, (1918), 54; E. C. Curwen, *Prehistoric Sussex*, (1929), 70, mentions a well 'said to have existed in the valley to the south [of Chanctonbury Ring], and was attributed to the Romans.

26 R. Milner-Gulland, 'The Washington Estate: New Evidence on an Ancient Boundary', *SAC* **143**, (2005), 205-14; WSRO, Ordnance Survey Map, Sheet 51, 1" to the mile, 1879 (1883), shows a Well House at TQ 1265 1130.

27 Field trip to former well site with Bob and Pamela Platt, using GPS and various maps, on 12 September 2011.

28 WSRO, Ordnance Survey Map, Sheet 51, 1" to the mile, 1879 (1883), clearly shows a pond at this spot.

29 WSRO, Wiston Mss 5517 (1).

30 WSRO, Wiston Mss 5517 (2).

31 WSRO, Wiston Mss 5517 (3).

32 WSRO, Wiston Mss 5517 (4).

33 J. M. L. Booker, (ed.), *The Wiston Archives, A Catalogue*, (1975), 234.

34 Current medical opinion is that the king suffered from porphyria, a rare hereditary disease that caused neurological damage and mental instability. After several months of illness 1788-1789, the king became ill again in 1810 and withdrew (or was withdrawn by his physicians) into a private 'mad' world until his death in 1820.

35 Prize Essay, by Charles Goring, 16 March 1802, details courtesy of Jane Goring Page and Joyce Sleight.

36 WSRO, Wiston Mss 5611-5638.

37 Booker, x; Mrs Patricia Gill completed the indexes by 1974, and other staff had taken part in the preliminary work. Mr Booker's words were echoed by Mr Stephen Freeth (ed.), *The Wiston Archives, Vol 2, A Catalogue*, (1982), vi. In 1990 I made a tape recording of Mr. John Goring's early memories and this can be found at WSRO, OH 86.

Chapter 2

1 P. Brandon, *The South Downs*, (1998), 9.

2 Personal comment in 1990.

3 Personal communication from Mr R. H. Goring.

4 Found by Bob Platt on 1 August 2010 and tentatively identified by him as 'Minerva's elbow or a piece of fossilised baguette...'; later confirmed as part of a Neolithic hammer stone by Luke Barber, Research Officer, Sussex Archaeological Society, Lewes, East Sussex.

5 G. S. Mitchell, 'Excavations at Chanctonbury Ring, 1909', SAC **53**, (1910), 131.

6 Personal comment by Mr R. H. Goring.

7 *West Sussex Gazette*, newspaper cutting dated '1978', in private hands.

8 *DNB*, article on Lawrence by Michael Levy; Ann Lawrence, the sister of Sir Thomas Lawrence (1769-1830), married the Revd Richard Rouse Bloxam, under master of Rugby School. Their son, the Revd Dr John Rouse Bloxam (1807-1891), became vicar of Upper Beeding, Sussex, from 1862 to his death in 1891. Lawrence himself never married, and in 1807 he had debts of more than £20,000. In 1810 he raised his portrait price of 200 guineas to 400 guineas when his chief competitor, John Hopper, portraitist, died. Charles Goring presumably paid 200 guineas for his portrait, escaping the doubling of the price one year later. Lawrence was knighted in 1815.

9 Letter from Dr P. Brandon to the *West Sussex Gazette*, 7.9.1989.

10 WSRO, Acc. No. 15920, ledger for 'Wiston Estate: Woods'.

11 'Chanctonbury's Trees', *SCM* 9, no. 12, (Dec. 1935), 739; J. Simpson, 'Legends of Chanctonbury Ring', *Folklore* **80**, (Summer 1969), 128.

12 *SCM* **10, no. 1**, (Jan. 1936), 83.

13 County Notes, 'Chanctonbury Ring', *SCM* 10, no. 1, (Jan. 1936), 88-89.

14 C. A. Grigg, *Memories of Steyning*, (1967), 28.

15 Personal communication from Mr R. H. Goring.

16 J. Simpson, 128.

17 O. Bedwin, 'Excavations at Chanctonbury Ring, Wiston, West Sussex 1977', *Britannia* **11**, (1980), 173, 175; Rudling, 78.

18 Personal communication from Mr R. H. Goring. The seed was raised at the Paddockhurst Estate, near Turners Hill, Sussex.

19 *West Sussex Gazette*, 'Future of Chanctonbury Ring assured', interview with Mr R. H. Goring by reporter Roy Affleck, 21.1.1988; letter from Dr P. Brandon, 7.9.1989; letter from J. Pennington, 21.9.1989

20 Personal communication from Mr R. H. Goring.

21 Brandon, (1998), 8-9, 149; note that the oil painting of Wiston House, c.1668, Plate IV, opp p 17 in Brandon's book has been printed back to front. Chanctonbury Hill is hidden behind the Holm oak tree which is on the left of the published picture, but should be on the right, i.e. to the west.

22 Brandon, (1998), 140.

23 Personal comment from Mr Richard Goring.

24 Letter from Dr P. Brandon to the *West Sussex Gazette*, 7.9.1989. The title of Stockwood's book is actually *Chanctonbury Ring*, and is discussed in Chapter 5.

Chapter 3

1 M. Tibble, 'A Topographical Survey of Chanctonbury Ring', *SAC* **146**, (2008), 71.

2 WSRO, Wiston Mss 5517 (1), draft letter dated 28 September 1786 from Charles Goring of Wiston to Roger Clough Esq. of Warminghurst, Sussex; at other times he writes 'Chankbury'.

3 T. P. Hudson, (ed.), *The Victoria County History*, 6, Pt 1, (1980), 260.

4 R. Milner-Gulland, 205-14.

5 D. Kingsley, 'Printed Maps of Sussex 1575-1900, *SRS* **72**, (1980-1981), 91-96.

6 R. Hewitt, *Map of a Nation: A Biography of the Ordnance Survey*, (2010), 103-04, 114, 130-37; with thanks to Pamela Platt for drawing my attention to this publication.

7 H. Smail, *The Worthing Road and Its Coaches* (1943), 12.

8 J. Evans, *Picture of Worthing, to which is added An Account of the Adjacent Villages, and of the Rides and Excursions in its Vicinity*, Vol. 1 (1814, 2nd edn), 114, 116; Vol. 2 (1814, 2nd edn), 27, 31; *The Gentleman's Magazine*, Vol. 89, (1819), 510.

9 WSRO, PM283, Draft Ordnance Survey 2" map, c. 1806-1807.

10 WSRO, Wiston Mss 5638, c.1825; see Kingsley, 177-184, for details of the Figg family of Lewes and their surveying practice.

11 Hudson, 247.

12 Letter (in private hands) from the Revd John Goring to his sister Elizabeth Trower, post-1861.

13 W. D. Cooper, 'Proofs of Age of Sussex Families, Temp. Edw. II to Edw. IV', *SAC* **12**, (1860), 28; A. Mawer & F. M. Stenton, (eds), *The Place-Names of Sussex*, Pt 1, (1929), 242; E. Ekwall, *The Concise Oxford Dictionary of English Place-Names*, (1960, 4th edn), 95.

14 L. F. Salzman, *The Chartulary of Sele*, (1923), 81 (no. 145) Ellis of Changethone; 55, (no. 104) Ralph de Changetone; 60 (no. 85) Clarice the widow of Waleran of Sengelton; 91 (no. 165) Sir Henry de Guldeford lord of Changeton; Mawer & Stenton, 53 Singleton: 'This difficult name is the same as Singleton, with a curious change of initial consonant', 242.

15 Richard Coates, Professor of Linguistics at the University of the West of England (formerly of the University of Sussex) is not sure about this, feeling that it looks like 'an original double name: *burg* at *Ceanc(el)* and *tun* at *Ceanc(el)*. *Ceanc(el)* would have been the original proper name of the hill (personal communication). Ekwall 74-75; M. Gelling, *Place-Names in the Landscape: The geographical roots of Britain's place-names*, (1993 edn), 127-28.

16 With grateful thanks to Richard Coates, for his help and advice; Mawer & Stenton, 242; F. Kitchen, 'The Ghastly War-Flame: Fire Beacons in Sussex until the Mid 17th Century', *SAC* **124**, (1986), 187-88.

17 R. Coates, *The traditional dialect of Sussex: A historical guide, description, selected texts, bibliography and discography*, (2010), 81; with thanks also to Richard Coates for alerting me to 'The South Downs and the Sussex Downs from Gorehill House, near Petworth with Chanklebury Ring', a drawing by Edward William Cooke dated 1876. Whether Cooke (1811-1880) knew Blunt is uncertain.

18 W. Figg, 'On the Remains of a Roman Building discovered at Wiston in 1848', *SAC* **2**, (1849), 313-15.

19 A. McWhirr, (ed.), *Roman Brick and Tile: Studies in Manufacture, Distribution and Use in the Western Empire*, (1979) 168-69.

20 J. Beck, 'Remarkable Discovery of Saxon Coins at Washington', *SAC* **19**, *Notes & Queries*, 189. I have not been able to discover the present whereabouts of these coins.

21 J. C. Lucas, 'The Hoard of Anglo-Saxon Coins Found at Chancton Farm, Sussex', *SAC* **20** (1868), 212-21.

22 Lucas, (1868), 213-14.

23 Untitled poem written by Charles Goring, 15 January 1802; the following paragraphs come from this source. With thanks to Jane Goring Page, and to Joyce Sleight for the transcription.

24 H. A. Lane Fox, 27-52; *DNB*, article on Pitt-Rivers by Mark Bowden.

25 M. Tibble, 'A topographical survey of Chanctonbury Ring, West Sussex: An Interpretation of the Prehistoric Landscape from the Neolithic to the Middle Iron Age', *SAC* **146** (2008), 55.

26 Candlin, (21 August 1980).

27 WSRO, Wiston Mss 5759, Agreement dated lst June 1906, ' ...between Charles Goring and George Sharman Mitchell...whereby the latter is appointed agent of the Wiston estates...'

28 G. S. Mitchell, 'Excavations at Chanctonbury Ring, 1909', *SAC* **53** (1910), 131-37 – the following section is extracted from Mitchell's article.

29 Mitchell presumably did not know of the hut and beacon site here during the Napoleonic Wars (see Chapter 5).

30 E. Curwen & E. C. Curwen, 'Some Roman Antiquities – Wiston, Chanctonbury, and Cissbury', *SAC* **63**, *Notes & Queries* (1922), 220-21.

31 R. Thurston Hopkins, *Sussex Pilgrimages*, (1927), 73.

32 Sussex Archaeological Society, Barbican House Museum, Lewes, with thanks to Chris Milburn; Kimmeridge Shale, often known as Blackstone, is a naturally occurring bituminous oil shale in the Dorset area and elsewhere, mined by the Romans, and polished to make jewellery and ornaments; the finds are listed as

A007.6.1; A0011.101.1; 126.12; 1947.9; with them is a label marked 'Chanctonbury Ring 1887' which does not seem to fit any of the finds.

33 Tibble, 53.

34 H. B. A. Ratcliffe-Densham, 'A Woman of Wessex Culture', *SAC* **106** (1968), 40-49.

35 Bedwin, 174.

36 Bedwin, 173; Cissbury hillfort contains numerous Neolithic flint mines within its 60 acre site.

37 Bedwin, 176.

38 See Bedwin, 190-94 for more details on Roman-British temples.

39 See D. Rudling, 'Roman-period Temples, Shrines and Religion in Sussex', in D. Rudling (ed.), *Ritual Landscapes of Roman South-East Britain*, (2008), 95-138, for further details of this subject.

40 Rudling, (2001), 118; Tibble, 71.

41 Rudling, (2001), 75-121; he also found more evidence for WWII activity.

42 Rudling, (2001), 111; with thanks to John Mills, Senior Archaeologist, WSCC, for guidance on archaeological dating (all dates are approximate).

43 'Chanctonbury Ring', *SCM* **24, no. 1** (Jan. 1950), 1.

44 E. Cecil Curwen, *The Archaeology of Sussex*, (1954, 2nd rev. edn), 74-75.

45 Rudling, (2001), 112.

46 Rudling, (2001), 112-13.

47 With thanks to Peter Drewett for clarification.

48 Rudling, (2001), 108, 113-18.

49 This boar figurine was deposited at Worthing Museum.

50 Mr. Derek Crush, now of Daylands Farm, Ashurst, found a small boar figurine (now lost) when he was at Locks Farm, Wiston. He thought it might have been a child's toy, and felt that it could almost '...have rolled down from Chanctonbury Ring' (personal comment).

51 Rudling, (2001), 115-18.

52 Rudling, (2008), 116. Rudling suggests that the findings of these various deposits at different parts of the Ring may indicate 'a much larger series of such zonal structured deposits [offerings], perhaps as at Gournay-sur-Aronde in northern Gaul'.

53 Rudling, (2001), 118.

54 Rudling, (2001), 118; Milner-Gulland thinks that a burial on the parish boundary would be very likely for a criminal or suicide (personal comment to author).

55 Tibble, 53-73; he mentions that the barrows and earthworks on Chanctonbury Hill were rescheduled by English Heritage in 1997.

56 Tibble, 71.

57 Tibble, 72.

58 Tibble, 71-72.

59 With thanks to Mr R. H. Goring, and Mr R. Goring for allowing examination of these finds, and to David Rudling for identifying the objects.

60 see www.britarch.ac.uk

61 see www.stonepages.com/news/

Chapter 4

1 The National Archives, C135/113/20, Proof of Age.

2 Cooper, 23-44. The following information is taken from this source.

3 He became John Plantaganet, 3rd earl of Kent (7.4.1330-26.12.1352).

4 Cooper, 28; he relates that another monk, straying from Boxgrove, near Chichester, was killed in the Manwood [now Manhood, near Selsey in West Sussex] '...affording no very strong evidence of monastic popularity', though he does not give a date for this incident; with many thanks to Christopher Whittick for the illustration and transcriptions.

5 I am most grateful to Christopher Whittick for looking at TNA, JUST 3/123, Gaol Delivery Roll for the period: there was no record of an indictment for this murder.

6 L. F. Salzman, *The Chartulary of Sele*, (1923), Charter 29, p.22. Part of Philip Falconer's six acres of land were '...in the furlong on the east of Stonberghe'. Milner-Gulland refers to 'stan beorge' or stone barrow, as being one of the boundary marks of Washington in AD 947, adjoining the Wiston boundary; Booker, 252; WSRO, Wiston Mss 5602, the house called The Falconers north of the Steyning-Washington road was built as the rectory in 1801.

7 R. Hutton, *The Stations of the Sun: A History of the Ritual Year in Britain*, (1996), see his chapter The Midsummer Fires, 311-21.

8 Hutton, 312-13; 'worship' in this sense would mean 'in honour of St John' (see Oxford English Dictionary for numerous meanings of the word 'worship').

9 Milner-Gulland, 209.

10 Leeds Museums and Galleries, 13/28a/53; the drawing is dated 12 February 1635 (1636 new dating). I am most grateful to LMG for allowing reproduction of this drawing.

11 Farrant, 11.

12 The year in England began on 25 March until 1752, and there is often confusion over dates before this time. In 1669, aged 62, Hollar went to Tangier with Howard of Castle Rising. He died on 25 March 1677, aged 70, in Westminster; *DNB*, article on Hollar by Robert D. Harding.

13 Farrant, 11-12, wonders if Hollar made the etchings before the earl of Arundel's death in 1646, 'on account of their association with the county of his ancestral home [at Arundel].

14 British Library Board, Maps*14485.(20.).

15 Hudson, 263.

16 Letter from Frank Kitchen to Eric Holden, received 21 May 1987. Holden was doing some research on the deserted farm settlement of Lower Buddington which is shown in both the Dunstall and the Hollar etchings. He corresponded with Kitchen, who had recently published his research on Sussex fire beacons.

17 Kitchen, (1986), 181, 186, 188; the following information on the history of fire beacons comes from Kitchen's research.

18 See F. Harrison & J. S. North, *Old Brighton, Old Preston, Old Hove*, (1937), 42-49 for more details on the French raids on Brighton in 1514 and 1545. The original drawing (Fig. 58 is a redrawn copy) is undated, and presumably done soon after the 1514 attack; the inscription "1545 July 37 Hen. VIII" on the original is thought to have been added later. The French attack on Brighton in 1545 did not cause any burning of the town.

19 Hudson, 247.

20 Hewitt, 131-33.

21 Evans, Vol.1, 114-15.

22 WSRO, Acc. No. 15920, 'Wiston Estate: Woods'.

23 Personal communication from Mr R. H. Goring.

24 *West Sussex County Times*, 22 July 1988.

Chapter 5

1 H. Belloc, *The Four Men: A Farrago*, (1952 reprint), 80-81.

2 Kipling, (1973), 214; Hudson, 247.

3 Evans, Vol. 2, 31-32.

4 Evans, Vol. 1, 114-15; Vol. 2, 34.

5 *The Gentleman's Magazine*, Vol. 89 (1819), 510-512, the following description is taken from this source; the Wrekin, perhaps the best known landmark in Shropshire, 1335 ft in height (407 m); Mont Cenis, Savoie, France, 6833ft in height (2083m) – perhaps a little poetic licence has been used here in comparison to Chanctonbury.

6 H. Smith, 'Select Society: or, a Week at Worthing', *The Worthing Parade*, **No. 2**, (1954), 21.

7 The editor of *The Worthing Parade*, 25, above, says 'From the local allusions it seems certain that the...narrative was based upon an actual visit to Worthing at the time indicated'; *DNB*, article on Smith by Fiona Robertson. Professor Robertson (personal communication) states that Smith was in France from 1821 to 1825 and she does not know of a visit to Worthing in 1822. Smith may have fictionalised a visit made perhaps a year or so before that date, with 1822 theatre references added to make the piece seem current. Interestingly, in the original publication, the *New Monthly Magazine*, 4, (1822), 431-34, Smith writes 'Changtonbury' (432-433), and it must be presumed that the unnamed editor of *The Worthing Parade* altered the spelling to Chanctonbury in 1954.

8 Letter in private hands from Elizabeth Trower to the Revd John Goring, 14-15 June 1866.

9 Hudson, 247.

10 Sir William Eden to the Revd John Goring, 4 May 1868, letter in private hands; Sir William Eden (1803-1873) of Windlestone Hall, Co. Durham, was grandfather to Sir Anthony Eden, Prime Minister 1955-57.

11 Louis J. Jennings, *Field Paths and Green Lanes in Surrey and Sussex*, (1884, 4th edn), 78; *DNB*, article on Jennings by H. C. G. Matthew.

12 Louis J. Jennings, *Rambles Among the Hills: In the Peak of Derbyshire and the South Downs*, (1880), illustration facing p.187.

13 Jennings, (1880), 187-88.

14 John Davey, Head Forester in 1978, mentioned larches as having been part of the Ring (see Chapter 2).

15 Jennings, 192.

16 Jennings, 193.

17 Jennings, 194-95.

18 R. D. Blackmore, *Alice Lorraine: A Tale of the South Downs* (undated reprint, c.1922), 16, 278-79, 313; *DNB*, article on Blackmore by Charlotte Mitchell.

19 W. Plomer, (ed.), *Kilvert's Diary 1870-1879: Selections from the Diary of the Rev. Francis Kilvert*, (1964 edn), p.255; the diaries were not published until 1938-40. Kilvert met Elizabeth Rowland two years after the visit to Chanctonbury, marrying her in 1879. He sadly died of peritonitis ten days after his honeymoon; *DNB*, article on Kilvert by A. L. Le Quesne, rev. Brenda Colloms.

20 *DNB*, article on Blunt by Elizabeth Longford; National Maritime Museum, PAE5529, 'The South Downs and the Sussex Downs from Gorehill House, near Petworth, with Chanklebury Ring', 1876, by Edward William Cooke.

21 Coates, 81; P. Anderson & K. McKenna, West Sussex Literary Trail, (2007), 38-41.

22 W. S. Blunt, *My Diaries: Being a Personal Narrative of events 1888-1914*, Pt 2, (5th edn, n.d.), 146.

23 Belloc, 79-80; *DNB*, article on Belloc by Bernard Bergonzi.

24 Belloc, 80-81.

25 Belloc, 124-33.

26 D. R. Banting, *William of Muntham: A Nabob of Sussex*, (1984), 5, 59; part of Belloc's drinking song is reproduced in this book, the Washington Inn being the *Frankland Arms*, whose sign records William Frankland (*c.* 1720–1805) of Muntham Court, near Findon.

27 Lucas, (1904), 145-46; *DNB*, article on Lucas by E. V. Knox, rev. Katharine Chubbock.

28 Lucas, 146-147; personal comment by Mr R. H. Goring.

29 The term '…was no Government Ale' in this poem perhaps dates the composition of Coombe's poems to c.1920 – this was the name given to the weak beer brewed from April 1917, when the strength and output of beer was lowered by Government war-time regulations.

30 *Rudyard Kipling's Verse, Inclusive Edition 1885-1926*, (1929, 4th impression), 483.

31 R. Kipling, 'They', (1905), 7.

32 Kipling, (1905), 8-9; *DNB*, article on Kipling by Thomas Pinney.

33 Kipling, (1905), 10-11; M. Smith, *Kipling's Sussex*, (2008), 55-56.

34 A. Beckett, *The Spirit of the Downs*, (1909), 158.

35 The poem was engraved on a stone placed in Mouse Lane in 2000. It was damaged by a lorry and removed to Steyning Museum; and a new engraving has taken its place in '…the lane that goes from Steyning to the Ring'. With thanks to Steyning Museum, where the original manuscript resides.

36 L. Denyer, *Steyning Museum Newsletter*, (October 2009), 3-6; (December 2009), 3-4; Purvis was ordained as a priest in 1933, leaving Cranleigh in 1938. He was appointed archivist to the archbishop and diocese of York in 1939, and in due course became a canon of York Minster. He translated the York Mystery Plays, for which he was awarded the OBE in 1958, and he organised the basic indexes of the two million documents in the York Diocese Archives.

37 Information from Mr Chris Tod, curator of Steyning Museum

38 E. Farjeon, *Martin Pippin in the Apple Orchard* , (1952 edn), 23-51; *DNB*, article on Farjeon by John Bell, rev. Victoria Miller.

39 Farjeon, 33

40 J. Galsworthy, *The Forsyte Saga: To Let*, (1921), pp.50, 60, 74-75, with thanks to both Ian Ivatt and Joyce Sleight of Steyning for bringing this chapter to my attention. Galsworthy bought a property at Bury in 1926 and lived there for most of the next seven years, though he died at his London house in 1933. His ashes were scattered by aeroplane over the South Downs on 3 February 1933, as requested in his will; *DNB*, article on Galsworthy by Geoffrey Harvey.

41 Personal communication from Pamela Platt.

42 With thanks to George Cockman of Steyning, whose research on Charles Dalmon is forthcoming.

43 A. Hadrian Allcroft, *Downland Pathways*, (1924, 2nd edn), 173-74; Allcroft explains that 'Heaven's Gate, corrupted to Hevends Gate, is a track that 'heaves' its way up to the summit of a hill. However, the term is more properly 'Heave-Gate', from the Anglo-Saxon Hefan and gaet, meaning a low gate so constructed as to lift out from the posts, instead of opening with hinges, see Coates, 137.

44 Hopkins, 44-45.

45 I. Lace, 'John Ireland' (1997), which can be seen on The John Ireland Charitable Trust website www.musicweb-international.com/ireland; *DNB*, article on Ireland by Fiona Richards.

46 F. Edwin Hodder, 'Chanctonbury', *SCM* **6, no. 9**, (Sept. 1932), 568. I have not been able to discover anything about Hodder, and would be grateful to have any information.

47 P. Gosse, *Go To The Country*, (1935), 72, 105-06; *DNB*, article on Gosse by Raymond Lister.

48 A. Mee, *Sussex: The Garden by the Sea*, (1937), 419.

49 A. Mee, *Sussex: The Garden by the Sea*, (1947 reprint), 390.

50 N. Price, *Jack By The Hedge*, (1942), excerpts reproduced in M. D. Francis (ed.), *The Sussex Bedside Anthology*, (1950), 269-27; *DNB*, article on Price by John Elsom.

51 Price, 271.

52 T. Newton, with C. Walker & A. Brown, *The Demonic Connection: An Investigation into Satanism in England and the International Black Magic Conspiracy*, (1987); with thanks to Sheila Wright of the Beeding & Bramber Local History Society for alerting me to this publication.

53 Simpson, 128.

54 Letter from Wendy Dixon to the author, 10th May 1994.

55 W. Dixon, 'When Canada Came to Help Britain', (1999), Steyning Museum Archives, WWII.

56 F. C. Dunford, *Chanctonbury Idylls*, (1947-1987), 87.

57 See Booker, Pedigree of the Goring Family, facing xiv.

58 Grigg, 27-28.

59 East Sussex Record Office, LIA/3/1, 2, Letter in the Attic project, one of 128 letters written by Eric Holden to Hilda whilst he was en route to, and stationed in, India in the Royal Engineers from April 1945 to February 1946; Hilda Holden wrote 87 letters in return.

60 Beckett, 158; Simpson, 122-31. Though could a dragon be substituted for the Devil? The word Wormstall in the AD 963 charter for Washington (see Chapter 3 and Fig. 35) probably means 'Dragon's Lair' and could refer to Chanctonbury Ring, see Milner Gulland, 209; Beckett, 131; the Devil's Dyke, another prehistoric earthwork, is not far away to the east of Chanctonbury Ring, and stories must have been circulating for centuries to explain the many 'humps and bumps' on the Downs.

61 M. Stockwood, *Chanctonbury Ring*, (1982), 93, 96, 99, photograph opposite 113, 206, 214; *DNB*, article on Stockwood by Michael De-la-Noy.

62 Brandon, (1998), 9.

Postscript

1 Tibble, 71.

2 The Hangleton Cottage at the Weald and Downland Open Air Museum, Singleton, near Chichester, West Sussex, is a reconstruction based on the excavation shown in Fig. 76.

Index

*'I am still employed in making an index – an occupation full as entertaining
as that of darning stockings, tho' by no means so advantageous to society'*
Gilbert White , 8 January 1788, letter to Sam Barker